THE ORDER

Confirmed
as children,

Affirmed
as teens

🔥 Font and Table Series

The *Font and Table Series* offers pastoral perspectives on
Christian baptism, confirmation and eucharist. Other titles in the series are:

A Catechumenate Needs Everybody: Study Guides for Parish Ministers

An Easter Sourcebook: The Fifty Days

At that Time: Cycles and Seasons in the Life of a Christian

Baptism Is a Beginning

Before and After Baptism: The Work of Teachers and Catechists

The Church Speaks about Sacraments with Children:
Baptism, Confirmation, Eucharist, Penance

Confirmation: A Parish Celebration

Finding and Forming Sponsors and Godparents

Guide for Sponsors

How Does a Person Become a Catholic?

How to Form a Catechumenate Team

Issues in the Christian Initiation of Children: Catechesis and Liturgy

Parish Catechumenate: Pastors, Presiders, Preachers

Welcoming the New Catholic

When Should We Confirm? The Order of Initiation

Related and available through Liturgy Training Publications:
The Rite of Christian Initiation of Adults (Ritual Edition)
The Rite of Christian Initiation of Adults (Study Edition)
Rito de la Iniciación Christiana de Adultos (Ritual Edition)

Confirmed as Children, Affirmed as Teens

THE ORDER OF INITIATION

Edited by James A. Wilde

Authors

Frank C. Quinn

•

Gerard Austin

•

Richard P. Moudry

•

David M. Beaudoin

•

Deborah Levine

•

James A. Wilde

•

J. Leo Klein

•

Carol and Larry Nyberg

•

Jacquelyn Mallory

LTP

Liturgy Training Publications

All references to the *Rite of Christian Initiation of Adults* (RCIA) are based on the text and the paragraph numbers of the 1988 edition: © 1985, International Committee on English in the Liturgy; © 1988, United States Catholic Conference.

Excerpts from *Guidelines for Sacramental Policies for the Archdiocese of Brisbane,* © 1989, Archdiocese of Brisbane. Used with permission. All rights reserved.

"Eucharist and the Confirmation Debate," Gerard Austin, is reprinted from *Catechumenate: A Journal of Christian Initiation* (January 1990) and "Celebration of Passage: Childhood to Adolescence," by David M. Beaudoin, is reprinted from *Catechumenate: A Journal of Christian Initiation* (September 1988).

"Bar Mitzvah: A Modern Perspective on Judaism's Rite of Passage," © 1990 Deborah Levine. Used with permission. All rights reserved.

"A Parish Resource for Confirmation: What Does Vatican II Say?" © 1989, Richard P. Moudry. Used with permission. All rights reserved.

Printed in the United States of America
Art: Linda Ekstrom
Design: Ana Aguilar-Islas
ISBN 0-929650-27-1

Contents

Introduction

JAMES A. WILDE

CHRISTIANS HAVE A RITE of passage called the paschal mystery. They celebrate it in the sacraments of initiation—baptism, confirmation and eucharist—whenever that passover takes place in life: infancy, childhood, adolescence, adulthood or on the deathbed. Through that rite of passage, persons become full participants with the apostles at the table of the Lord.

Various societies have other rites of passages: For some, puberty marks a passage. Others associate "coming of age" with graduation. Still others connect the passage with driving a car, drinking, making an apostolic commitment, voting, professing religious vows, fighting in war, reconciling, marrying or even owning land or a home. Some people consider the death of one's parent or spouse as a time of passage. For Christians, however, these biological, social, cultural or religious passages are *rehearsals* or *encores* of the passover in Christ. Dying and rising with Christ gives a home, a meaning and a direction to all other human passages.

1

When Should We Confirm?

Since the publication of *When Should We Confirm? The Order of Initiation* (Chicago: Liturgy Training Publications, 1989), we note happily that many more dioceses and parishes in Canada, the United States and abroad are restoring the traditional order of initiatory sacraments: baptism, confirmation, eucharist. True, a new conservatism has eroded some of the work of Vatican II, but the pioneering leadership of pastors such as Richard P. Moudry, bishops such as Patrick Kelly and archbishops such as Anthony Bevilacqua and John R. Roach, as reported in that book, has not passed unnoticed.

The guidelines for confirmation in the Roman Catholic archdiocese of Brisbane, under the leadership of Francis R. Rush, archbishop, exemplify one especially practical approach:

CONFIRMATION IS CELEBRATED TOGETHER WITH, OR PRIOR TO, THE FIRST RECEPTION OF EUCHARIST. The custom of the Roman Rite is to complete the initiation of those baptized as infants when they have reached the use of reason. Eucharist is the climax of the initiation process. Hence, in order to respect our theological and liturgical tradition, confirmation is celebrated prior to the first reception of eucharist.

Because the *Rite of Christian Initiation of Adults* provides a model for sacramental initiation, it is appropriate that this completion of initiation be seen as a single process involving the renewal of baptismal promises, sealing with the gift of the Spirit (confirmation) and introduction to the eucharistic table.

It is desirable that the bishop not only confirm the child but also give the child first holy communion. This affirms the unity of the sacraments of initiation and highlights their orientation toward and climax in the celebration of eucharist. It also properly focuses on the bishop as leader of the eucharistic community.

When it is not practicable for a bishop to celebrate this completion of children's initiation with the parish community, express delegation of the pastor or another priest may be granted on application, in accordance with the provisions of canon 884.

Because the child's confirmation and first eucharist relate so intimately to baptism, it is desirable that the baptismal sponsors be involved with the parents and child in the parish sacramental preparation program (see canon 893). This provides a privileged pastoral opportunity for all involved to renew their commitment to the child's continued faith growth and practice.

Children who already have made their first communion but have not been confirmed may be presented for confirmation on the next occasion that the sacrament is offered. Parishes will need to arrange an appropriate preparation program during the period of transition to this new diocesan practice.

At the parish level, the experience of St. Ephrem Church, Sterling Heights, Michigan, under the leadership of Robert H. Blondell, affords a noteworthy example. In that experience, the well-orchestrated synchrony of catechesis and liturgy, along with the apostolic work of unusually large numbers of parishioners, gave the children who celebrated their confirmation and first communion at Easter 1990 something to remember. The logistics of sacramental catechesis for the additional 650 children and teens who completed their sacramental initiation through the celebration of confirmation at the same time—not to mention the catechesis for their parents and godparents—awakened thousands of men, women and children to a new and exciting time in the church.

Confirmed as Children

The authors of this volume know that the restoration of the order of initiation can take place in many ways, some more appropriate than others. There is as yet no one model that applies to all people. Nor does the restoration of the order in any way imply that the church sanctifies one age—for example, age seven or even general adulthood—over others. We recognize that there are some real questions about some of the initiatory rites, not the least of which is the weakness of the texts and ritual action of confirmation (for example, a "laying on of hands" without physical touch). We do not pretend that this book is the last word on the subject. But we do attempt to ask central questions and to place the issue in the appropriate context.

Frank C. Quinn, OP, professor of liturgy at Aquinas Institute, St. Louis, Missouri, shows how, especially since the sixteenth century, confirmation has had several meanings and functions. Sorting out these functions ranks first on the list of priorities. Can we face the possibility that sacraments are not carrots or rewards for education?

Gerard Austin, OP, professor of pastoral liturgy at The Catholic University of America, Washington, and author of *Anointing with the Spirit: The Rite of Confirmation and the Use of Oil and Chrism,* examines the particular relation between the eucharist and confirmation. The context in which Austin situates the current and future discussion about confirmation does justice both to the knowns and to the unknowns of the sacrament.

Richard P. Moudry, pastor of Christ the King Church, Crystal, Minnesota, documents the coherent teaching of the church on confirmation since the Vatican II. His citation of official texts and his careful commentary on them disclose a consistency in church teaching and pastoral practice that may surprise some readers.

Affirmed as Teens

A religious educator, David M. Beaudoin, consultant for the office of Catholic education, archdiocese of Chicago, examines the catechetical and liturgical principles appropriate for a child in the seventh, eighth or ninth grade. He finds in the church calendar rich fare for the boy or girl around 13 years old to experience and articulate.

Deborah Levine, of the Chicago chapter of the American Jewish Committee, frankly reveals some of the values and problems of the bar and bat mitzvah for contemporary Jews. Christians may learn much from this tradition of Judaism, especially as it relates to young Jewish men and women not as groups but as individuals.

The promulgation of the *Rite of Christian Initiation of Adults* marks the dawn of a new era for teens, according to James A. Wilde. The few child or adult teens who pass through Christian initiation can occasion a new, powerful vision of Christ and the church not only for themselves but for all their peers.

J. Leo Klein, SJ, professor of theology, Xavier University, Cincinnati, Ohio, proves beyond a doubt that absolutely nothing can be assumed regarding the faith of young people, that sacraments never must be routine and that church leaders and educators must learn to listen much better to youth. Klein's remarkably sensitive ten-year "experiment" in a university setting helps affirm unbaptized believers, baptized agnostics and all the others.

The *Book of Common Prayer* and the *Book of Occasional Services* of the Episcopal church give catechists and liturgists Carol and Larry Nyberg, Wheaton, Illinois, the foundation for a process and a rite that suits youth well. Grounded in scripture and in liturgical traditions of *anamnesis* and *epiclesis,* the Nybergs' approach to formation and celebration rekindles for teens the gifts of Christian initiation and disposes them to apostolic work.

Jacquelyn Mallory, pastoral associate and family catechist, St. Petersburg, Florida, thinks the *reconciliation* rather than *confirmation* more suits the realities of life for teens. The way teens experience both alienation and reconciliation makes them some of the finest "ambassadors of reconciliation" (2 Corinthians 5:20) in the domestic church, their peer church, the school church and the parish church.

Confirmation: Which One Should I Choose?

FRANK C. QUINN

You called me, Father, by my name
when I had still no say:
today you call me to confirm
the vows my parents made.[1]

T HE "HYMN FOR CONFIRMATION," quoted here, is intended for the rite of confirmation in several Protestant churches in which the candidates ratify the baptismal promises made in their name by parents/godparents at the time of baptism. The hymn's sentiments are in perfect accord not only with the modern Protestant view of confirmation but also with the sixteenth-century reformers' ideas of what confirmation, as conclusion to catechism study, should be about: publicly articulated and personal appropriation of baptism's demands.

This view of confirmation is at variance with the meaning the Catholic church assigns to the sacrament of confirmation. Ironically, I doubt that many Catholics, considering the way the sacrament has been practiced and preached in recent times, would consider the hymn's sentiments foreign to their notion of the rite. This is unfortunate because it adds to the confusion over confirmation as a sacrament normatively occurring between baptism and eucharist and confirmation as a catechetical rite of personal renewal, celebrated publicly before the assembly but only long after initiation has been completed.

If we could acknowledge that *confirmation* is a term referring to a number of quite different ecclesial rites and if we could agree that historically the rites parading under that term have different purposes and goals, we might be able to discuss the various issues that engage liturgists and catechists relative to the way sacraments of initiation versus rituals of renewal are to be practiced in the Roman church. In this chapter, we will explore these differences and make some suggestions for contemporary practice.

One Word, Many Rites

Confirmation does not refer to one ritual reality. History tells us that there are at least three ritual practices to which the word may apply: (1) the ancient episcopal postbaptismal part of the baptism rite, now restored in the new *Rite of Christian Initiation of Adults* (RCIA); (2) the medieval sacrament of confirmation, the postbaptismal rite separated from baptism and identified as an individual sacrament by Peter Lombard and later scholastics, later defined as such by the Council of Trent; and (3) the catechetical rite concluding catechism instruction that appeared in the reformation churches from the sixteenth century on. Each of these rites has been called confirmation.

THE EPISCOPAL POSTBAPTISMAL RITE

It is anachronistic to use *confirmation* for the episcopal postbaptismal rite because the word appeared long after that particular part of the baptismal liturgy was well established. It also is clear, however, why Catholics do speak of the conclusion of baptism as confirmation: The medieval rite, identified as one of the seven sacraments, evolved from the earlier episcopal rite that concluded baptism. Thus, the church insists in its rites for the initiation of adults that baptism conclude with the sacrament of confirmation; the ancient and relatively simple anointing by the bishop after baptism is no longer so simple. The RCIA presents a more complex rite of confirmation to make clear that a *new* sacrament is being celebrated, one supposedly distinct theologically from baptism. But in elaborating confirmation, the RCIA downplays the important postbaptismal rites, especially presbyterial chrismation. These now are called "Explanatory Rites" (RCIA, 227). The chrismation is omitted (228) if confirmation follows—which it normally must (227).

Still, the union of baptism and confirmation in RCIA, no matter what explanations are given, puts an end to the question of what confirmation is in the Catholic church. The problems arising from the practice of confirmation as a sacrament totally separate from baptism simply do not arise in this case.

THE MEDIEVAL SEPARATED RITE

The second form of confirmation, the medieval sacrament, is a rite searching for a theology, as writers have been fond of saying. This form of confirmation, separated from baptism and eucharist, has been the practice in the United States and Canada. It has in recent years been administered to adolescents between ages 12 and 16. Suggestions for variations in the practice have raised considerable conflict between those who begin with a liturgical perspective and those who begin with a catechetical perspective. Liturgists emphasize confirmation's role in initiation and its relation to baptism and eucharist. Often catechists promote the rite as the conclusion to an adolescent or adult faith journey (the hymn stanza quoted at the beginning of this chapter suits this interpretation).

The 1971 *Rite of Confirmation* (RC) reflects an attempt to play for both camps. It has elements of the conclusion to baptism that we find in the contemporary adult initiation rites. It likewise incorporates such additions as the baptismal credal questions—now four instead of three, because the third one from the rite of baptism is divided. This division of one question into two has the effect of focusing on belief in the Holy Spirit and the coming of the Holy Spirit—for the first time?—on the confirmands (RC, 23: "Do you believe in the Holy Spirit . . . who . . . today is given to you sacramentally in confirmation?"). These questions, along with the "model" homily insisting on the new outpouring of the Spirit at the bishop's hands, focus on a candidate's entry into an "adult," full relationship with the church and a candidate's personal, public acceptance of Jesus Christ—supposedly for the first time.

The relation of confirmation to baptism and eucharist is emphasized repeatedly in the Apostolic Constitution on the sacrament of confirmation by Paul VI in 1971. In the general and specific pastoral introductions to the rite, as well as in the rubrics, this understanding is largely ignored because eucharist has been received long before confirmation, in effect already concluding initiation. In other words, there really is no way one can speak of separate confirmation as sealing baptism and leading to the real conclusion of initiation, the solemn first eucharist, if the latter already has occurred. In this case, the ceremonial first "postconfirmation" eucharist is both symbolically unconvincing and ritually anticlimactic.

Part of the problem with the medieval sacrament, of course, is the theology developed to explicate it, a theology founded, as is now well known, on the fifth-century homilies of an obscure semi-Pelagian bishop, Faustus of Riez, as well as on fragments of commentaries on the postbaptismal episcopal rites by Alcuin and his student, Rabanus Maurus. The homiletic musings of Faustus were believed to be the statements of several popes. That misunderstanding encouraged the belief that his remarks were more important theologically than they really were. But his comments offered a way of distinguishing the separate rite of confirmation from baptism: the images of strength, maturity, soldier, added grace. These ensured its place among the seven sacraments. Still, from a Catholic sacramental perspective, the medieval explanation of confirmation was better suited to that new form of confirmation that would appear in the sixteenth century than it was to the postbaptismal rite of patristic times.

CATECHETICAL RITE

Catechetical confirmation was a creation of the reformers, a ceremonial conclusion to the study of the catechism, undertaken by those who had been baptized as infants—the normal situation in western Europe. The fact that this rite occurred between infant baptism and eucharist (also not received until adolescence) made it look somewhat like the Roman sacrament of confirmation. (Until 1910, the Roman rite of confirmation preceded first eucharist, usually at age 12 to 14.) The various rituals make it clear that the reformers held different theories about their confirmation. Still, the confirmation created by the reformers (which, to be sure, they insisted was in no way a sacrament) differed considerably from the earlier two forms of confirmation. It was indeed a catechetical rite.

Toward Clarification of Terms

Today, all three *confirmations* exist side by side. No wonder the confusion and the need for clarification! After all, in the heyday of Christian initiation, the postbaptismal episcopal rites were only part of baptism, except in particular emergency situations. By the time confirmation emerged as an individual sacramental rite, separate from baptism, the postbaptismal episcopal rite no longer existed. And when the reformers created their catechetical rite, they were reacting not only to the then universal practice of infant baptism but also to the Roman practice of the then separate sacrament of confirmation.

Confusion continues today. The RCIA is normative for Roman Catholic practice, yet separate confirmation continues because, in many places, infants are baptized but not confirmed. And the reformers' catechetical rite has reemerged as a repeatable adult rite of affirmation that responds to a number of modern situations in church life. Adding to the confusion, the separate Catholic rite of confirmation now functions much as the reformers' and contemporary Protestant rite of confirmation/affirmation.

Catholics and Protestants long have disagreed over whether confirmation is a sacrament. The reformers created a new rite that had little to do with the medieval sacrament and was intended as a departure from the Roman practice, which many of them considered blasphemous. Little wonder neither side could admit the validity of the other's rite! Thus, rather than listening to each other, acknowledging the rich variety in practice and benefiting from successes and failures, Catholics and Protestants usually have turned a deaf ear to one another and continued to rehearse the sixteenth-century battles.

Learning from One Another

But what if we can learn from one another? What if the new rites of affirmation created by, among others, the Episcopal and Lutheran churches, also point to a solution to some of the problems in Catholic practice, where so often the rite of confirmation is demeaned by forcing it to play the impossible role of testifying to authentic adult conversion?

Both Lutheran and Episcopal churches in America have looked at their rites of confirmation with fresh eyes. They have attempted to make clear distinctions between ancient rites that conclude baptism and admit to eucharist and newer rites that mark special times after initiation is completed. These latter rites are for occasions when particular individuals feel called to affirm their faith before the liturgical assembly.

The newly reformed rites of baptism in these churches now contain such postbaptismal elements as laying on of hands and anointing (not called confirmation). Their rites of confirmation, affirmation or reaffirmation are repeatable, inspired by the reformation rites of catechetical confirmation, providing various forms for an explicit, public profession of faith.[2] Though inspired by reformation practice, these rites are particularly modern because today we realize that our postbaptismal journey to resurrection is made up of many types of conversion or affirmation.[3]

For Catholics, one might say that there always is the sacrament of penance as a rite of renewal. But one then must ask why the Catholic sacrament of confirmation is being manipulated to produce what Lutherans and Anglicans hope to achieve by their "nonsacramental" rites of affirmation.[4] Perhaps beyond penance there is a need to develop rites that make public affirmation of faith before a bishop and the local community possible.

Once we can distinguish between sacraments and rites of affirmation, there is no problem with allowing ourselves to be influenced concerning these rites by our fellow churches. In this way, we can avail ourselves of rites of affirmation that respond to contemporary needs and, at the same time, protect the initiatory role of confirmation by replacing it as the conclusion to baptism and the gate to the eucharistic table.

Conclusion

We should respect the authentic tradition of the church and simply restore what we call the sacrament of confirmation to its position immediately after baptism, whenever the latter is celebrated. The eucharist in the authentic tradition of the church completes baptism/ confirmation, whenever the latter is celebrated. The one difference between ancient and contemporary practice, of course, would be that because the bishop is no longer the *ordinary* minister of baptism, he also no longer will be the *ordinary* minister of confirmation. In this way, fruitless debates between catechists and liturgists can come to an end and both groups can give thought to what postbaptismal formation implies and how various rites of conversion benefit contemporary life.

The need for such rites of affirmation already has been discussed in a brief but important pamphlet from the U.S. Bishops' Committee on the Liturgy, *Christian Commitment.*[5] The need to live out baptismal faith and to renew it on occasion, beyond the initiatory sequence of baptism-confirmation-eucharist and beyond the rite of penance, is given expression in this pamphlet. The authors speak of the many moments for renewal already found in our liturgies and seasons, whether at weekly eucharist or in the sacraments of healing and status (such as anointing, penance, marriage and orders), as well as in the rite of religious profession and at moments such as the renewal of baptismal vows in the Easter Vigil. These ritual occasions provide opportunities for personal recommitment. But what about specific rites of renewal or affirmation that correspond to personal needs not all that satisfactorily expressed in our liturgy, specific rites that afford personal affirmation before the gathered assembly? Perhaps we do need, on the model of the Lutheran and Episcopal churches, to develop official rites of affirmation that Catholics are able to celebrate at various moments in the course of life.

The joining together and celebrating of baptism-confirmation-eucharist, whenever baptism is allowed, would restore the church's authentic initiatory traditions. It also would enable us to focus our attention on that which is crucial to authentic sacramental praxis: the Christian formation of those sacramentally initiated in infancy. Instead of creating an artificial confirmation catechumenate, we could focus on the fact that, having celebrated the order of Christian initiation according to the authentic traditions, we now must provide a spiritual and religious formation that ensures that the sacraments have not been offered in vain.

It seems to me that these procedures—though certainly not a panacea—will ensure a more robust sacramentality as well as a more authentic catechesis.

Notes

1. "A Hymn for Confirmation," text by Fred Kaan, Hymn Concerto Series, (Carol Stream, Illinois: Hope Publishing Company, 1979), 8.

2. See "Affirmation of Baptism," *Lutheran Book of Worship* (Minneapolis: Augsburg Publishing House, 1978), 198–201; "Confirmation with Forms for Reception and for the Reaffirmation of Baptismal Vows," *The Book of Common Prayer and Administration of the Sacraments and Other Rites and Ceremonies of the Church, According to the Use of the Episcopal Church* (New York: The Church Hymnal Corporation, 1979), 412–19. Unfortunately, the first of these rites still is called confirmation rather than affirmation. It is considered to be the first public articulation of baptismal faith. As such, it is, of course, unrepeatable. But it also is clear that this rite of "confirmation" is not part of the baptism-eucharist initiation.

3. For a fuller examination of these rites, see Gerard Austin, *The Rite of Confirmation: Anointing with the Spirit,* Studies in the Reformed Rites of the Catholic Church 3 (New York: Pueblo Publishing Company, 1985), 65–88. See also my article, "Confirmation, Does It Make Sense?" *Ecclesia Orans* (1988), 321–40.

4. It also should be noted that the revised Lutheran and Episcopal liturgies include separate rites of confession and forgiveness. Therefore, it is clear their rites of affirmation address issues other than penance and reconciliation.

5. U.S. Bishops' Committee on the Liturgy, *Christian Commitment* (Washington: United States Catholic Conference, 1978); cf. also Austin's comments on this document in *The Rite of Confirmation: Anointing with the Spirit,* 134–35.

Eucharist and the Confirmation Debate

GERARD AUSTIN

N O OTHER SACRAMENT has had such a turning and twisting road throughout its history than the sacrament of confirmation. The Second Vatican Council did not have a lot to say about this sacrament, but by far the most important thing it did say was in the *Constitution on the Sacred Liturgy*, 71: "The rite of confirmation is to be revised in order that the intimate connection of this sacrament with the whole of Christian initiation may stand out more clearly." This statement contextualizes the problem. It clearly places confirmation in its proper setting as one of the initiation sacraments. The 1983 *Code of Canon Law* did the same thing in canon 842: "The sacraments of baptism, confirmation and the most holy eucharist are so interrelated that they are required for full Christian initiation." Still, the debate goes on, and pastoral practice, at least in the majority of cases, continues to belie the initiatory context of confirmation and continues to celebrate it long after the celebration of first eucharist.

Before Christian Baptism

The story of confirmation begins, of course, with baptism, but where does the story of Christian baptism begin? God did not pull Christian sacraments out of a magician's hat, totally without connection to anything known at that particular time in history. This brings us to the question of the antecedents of Christian initiation, to pre-Christian religious water rituals.

A study of the evidence reveals that the use of water for purificatory purposes is a common phenomenon of religions. In many religions there is a tendency to concentrate purification in one important rite near the time of a person's birth.

Water is used because of its symbolism. Historians of religion like Mircea Eliade tell us that water symbolizes all potentiality. It is formlessness. Reentry into formlessness purifies and regenerates, for it nullifies the past and restores, even if only for a time, the integrity of the dawn of things.

The Jewish roots of Christian baptism begin with various ritual washings of defiled objects or clothing and culminate in the message of the prophets. Ezekiel speaks of a bath to be given by God: "I will sprinkle clean water upon you, and you shall be clean from all your uncleanness, and from all your idols I will cleanse you" (Ezekiel 36:25). Many see this text to be of capital importance. With Ezekiel we pass from the bath given to oneself to that given by God or by God's chosen minister.

There was another type of water ritual used by the Jewish communities: proselyte baptism whereby a gentile became a Jewish convert. Just how much proselyte baptism influenced Christian baptism is a matter of debate. The influence probably was more on the level of theology than on the level of ritual.

Water and the Spirit

Important for understanding the development of Christian baptism is the water rite of John the Baptizer, especially as it is experienced by Jesus himself. Jesus' baptism by John serves as a revelation of the mystery of salvation in Jesus. Jesus is baptized not for his own sins but for the sins of others. He is baptized in view of his death, which will cause the Spirit of forgiveness to be given to the church. The Jordan event, Jesus' baptism by John, sets the tone for the way Christian initiation is understood. Just as Jesus was anointed with the Spirit in the Jordan, so his followers are anointed with the same Spirit. The water bath of conversion is primarily an event of the Spirit.

This relationship between water and Holy Spirit is key for understanding Christian initiation. The tradition is clear. Water is subordinated to Spirit, not vice versa. Unfortunately, in the historical development of the initiation sacraments there has been at times a subordination of Spirit to water, and this has caused an overemphasis on the water bath, cutting it off from its other ritual components such as anointings and laying on of hands. I would argue that the entire complex history of the relationship between baptism and confirmation reduces itself to the varying views of this relationship between "water" and "the Spirit." The immersion in water must not be isolated from the action of the Spirit or from the actions of faith and conversion of the baptizands. All these diverse elements must be held together in tension to avoid an impoverished understanding of the full mystery that is being accomplished.

In the early church the Spirit was seen to be given for the remission of sins and the bringing to life of "new creatures" in Christ. This was not the task of the water rite alone. Scripture scholar Raymond Brown has written:

> It would seem that New Testament thought is not rigorously consistent on the action that brings about the remission or cleansing of sin and Christian renewal. Many passages attribute such power to baptism, but many (without doing away with baptism) attribute it to other factors like faith and preaching. Perhaps we may say that preaching, repentance, faith and baptism were all involved in the New Testament concept of the remission of sins, and that the question of precisely how much of that remission should be attributed to baptism taken in isolation is a question of post–New Testament theology. ("We Profess One Baptism for the Forgiveness of Sins," *Worship* [May 1966], 271)

Often the confusion arises in texts from the Acts of the Apostles. We find many patterns of initiation in Acts. At times the Spirit is given at the moment of the water rite, at times at the moment of the laying on of hands and at times by the preaching of the word prior to the water rite. In one case (Acts 8) baptism in the name of Jesus is administered by Philip to the Samaritan but is not accompanied by the gift of the Holy Spirit. This creates a problem for a Pauline understanding of baptism. In Paul's eyes the Spirit is the fundamental mark of belonging to Christ, and the gift of the Spirit is the result of baptism. For Paul, sacramental dying and rising with Christ is one reality, and it brings about union with the Spirit *(pneuma)*-Christ. In light of this, many scholars argue that the New Testament offers no ground for a distinction between baptism and confirmation and that confirmation as a separate sacrament is a post—New Testament problem.

Confirmation as a Separate Sacrament

The early church was primarily concerned with making Christians, what we call today initiation. The principal ritual element for this was the water rite, but very early in Roman usage a rite reserved to the bishop was added: a postbaptismal chrismation. In fifth-century southeast Gaul, it acquired the name "confirmation." Interestingly, it was so termed in a context where this episcopal rite of confirmation was no longer part of baptism itself. The priest baptized, and then later on, the bishop "supplied the Spirit."

Confirmation as a separate sacrament tended to impoverish the meaning of the previous baptismal act and overstressed the importance of the presence of the bishop. The insistence on the presence of the bishop eventually overshadowed the traditional order of the initiation sacraments. This was the case in the West only, as the East continued to insist on the traditional order of the sacraments: baptism, chrismation, eucharist. The Eastern churches would see the presence of the bishop in the chrism that had been consecrated by him. At any rate, for them the traditional order was the greater good.

The West not only continued to delay confirmation until some time after baptism, it continued to pile onto the shoulders of confirmation new layers of meaning: increase of grace, power to preach to others, spiritual maturity and strength for battle in the Christian life. The Protestant reformers viewed "confirmation" as the ratification by an adult of the baptismal promises made on one's behalf when one was still an infant. As such it was viewed more as a "catechetical" rite, sort of a Christian bar mitzvah. This certainly was a break with the earlier tradition.

Unheeded Appeals by the Vatican

In 1774, the Congregation for the Propagation of the Faith issued an instruction for priests on the missions, allowing them to confirm, and this instruction was reproduced in all rituals until 1925. A delay until the seventh year was spoken of, but the minister could and should confirm earlier if there was any danger to the life of the child or a chance that a valid minister might not be available in the future, for then the child would be deprived of a great glory in heaven.

In 1897, Pope Leo XIII wrote a celebrated letter to the archbishop of Marseilles. This letter served as the immediate source for the 1917 *Code of Canon Law* concerning the age for confirmation and first communion. The pope argued that children need the grace given in confirmation even in their tender years, for it better prepares them to receive the eucharist.

This type of plea continued from Rome. In 1932, the Sacred Congregation for the Sacraments stated that it was in conformity with the nature of the sacrament of confirmation that children should not come to first communion until they received confirmation.

In 1952, the Commission for Interpreting the *Code of Canon Law* denied to a group of local bishops the power to delay confirmation until children were ten years old. They considered that too long a delay. Ten years old was too old. Again, this legislation went unheeded in most parts of the world.

In 1972, the *Rite of Christian Initiation of Adults* (RCIA) placed confirmation in the context of baptism and eucharist, that is, full Christian initiation:

> In accord with the ancient practice followed in the Roman liturgy,
> adults are not to be baptized without receiving confirmation
> immediately afterward, unless some serious reason stands in the way.
> The conjunction of the two celebrations signifies the unity of the
> paschal mystery, the close link between the mission of the Son and the
> outpouring of the Holy Spirit, and the connection between the two
> sacraments through which the Son and the Holy Spirit come with the
> Father to those who are baptized. (RCIA, 215)

The *Rite of Confirmation* (RC), when treating of children baptized in infancy, states that "the administration of confirmation is generally postponed until about the seventh year." But then it adds: "For pastoral reasons, however, especially to strengthen in the life of the faithful complete obedience to Christ the Lord in loyal testimony to him, episcopal conferences may choose an age which appears more appropriate, so that the sacrament is conferred after appropriate formation at a more mature age" (RC, 11).

Our U.S. bishops voted "that the norm of the *Ordo Confirmationis* be adopted in this country without further modification, saving the right of any ordinary who might wish to set a later age as normative in his jurisdiction." In practice, the norm of the *Ordo* (conferring confirmation at the age of about seven) is rarely the guideline used because currently most dioceses in the United States choose to confirm at a later age.

This option of delaying confirmation to a later age seems to change the whole focus of the sacramental action from baptismal grace to the baptized person, that is, from who we are (those loved gratuitously by God) to what we do (respond to that love). Furthermore, in choosing a later age for confirmation, is more not being demanded for confirmation than is demanded for the apex of Christian initiation, the eucharist itself? While young children are allowed to receive the greatest of all the Christian sacraments, the eucharist, they are denied confirmation.

More important, by delaying the age of confirmation, have we not turned the sacrament from the purpose for which it was instituted? Have we not changed confirmation from its original role as the completion and perfection of baptism (and as the gift of the fullness of the Spirit preparing for the reception of the body and blood of Christ) into something totally new: a catechetical rite concluding religious education and stressing in that context a personal, mature ratification of one's earlier baptism?

The Future of the Confirmation Debate

There will be no uniform confirmation practice in the immediate future. More and more parishes will elect for confirmation on the occasion of first eucharist, although this will be very slow in coming. That practice eventually will emerge as standard.

Meanwhile, the important thing is that the followers of the different schools of thought neither call each other names nor stereotype each other's positions.

Another caution is that we not make too much out of confirmation. A rather minor sacrament in our tradition is getting quite a lot of attention today, perhaps too much. Our major sacraments are baptism and eucharist. Baptism incorporates one into the body of Christ, and eucharist builds up the unity of that body. Baptism and eucharist mold all life in the church and determine the roles of the other sacraments. The sacrament of confirmation must not be an exception to this. Currently, many pay more attention to confirmation than to baptism, and often more preparation is demanded for confirmation than for eucharist itself. We forget that eucharist is the summit of the spiritual life and the goal of all the sacraments, as Thomas Aquinas put it, and that eucharist makes the church, as Cyprian stated.

We are baptized but once, confirmed but once. But eucharist we celebrate time after time, Sunday after Sunday, year after year. It is eucharist that our Bishops' Committee on the Liturgy called the "repeatable sacrament of initiation" (*Newsletter* 14 [1978]: 111). We often view confirmation as the conclusion of a process that heralds entry into mature membership in the church—a big order for a single event! Could more of our effort go into an ongoing process that involves our saying "yes" to baptism (to who we are as the body of Christ) Sunday after Sunday as we celebrate God's greatest gift to us, the eucharist? God has not only saved us once and for all through the sacrifice of Jesus but has willed that we ourselves as members of the body of Christ become "spiritual sacrifices acceptable to God through Jesus Christ" (1 Peter 2:5).

As St. Augustine put it: "You [the newly initiated] are there on the Lord's table; you are actually present in the chalice. You form this mystery with us." Why? Because we have put on Christ through the sacraments of initiation: baptism, confirmation, eucharist. Through our initiation we have become the body of Christ and through each repeated eucharist we become all the more what we already are. That is why and how we can offer ourselves to God in union with Christ, Sunday after Sunday, until it is all brought to completion and confirmed in death.

Thomas Aquinas stated that each act of charity is more intense than the previous one because it has the momentum of the previous act behind it. He likened it to the physical law of a falling body. This law is most aptly applied to the church's supreme act of love, the act of eucharist. Each eucharist is more intense than the previous one because we have the momentum of previous eucharistic actions behind it. The Christian life is an ongoing process, a continuing reaffirmation of who we are.

Catechesis is more than preparation for sacraments. It is tied into the ongoing life of the Christian: service and mission.

There is an analogy here with marriage. As important as the day of marriage is, what realistically is at the core of Christian marriage is the day-by-day "yes" to that initial commitment. It is the same with initiation. Initiation is a process. Baptized into Christ, anointed with the Spirit, it is in the eucharist that we repeatedly lay the gifts of our life on the altar with the bread and the wine, that those gifts may be transformed into the body and blood of Christ. This is not something that we do once and for all.

The initiation sacraments have to do primarily with unity: unity with the head and unity with the members of the body of Christ. But this initiation process is marked by an imperfect unity. We are not yet fully one with Christ the head, nor with one another, the members of

Christ's body. We ever seek a more perfect unity. This quest is what Christian life is all about.

The principal source of our growing in this unity is the eucharist, not just our first eucharist but the eucharist celebrated and lived throughout life.

A Parish Resource for Confirmation: What Does Vatican II Say?

RICHARD P. MOUDRY

I N THE 1960S AND 1970S, the children of our parish were confirmed at the seventh-grade level. When we considered changing
that practice, I wondered what Vatican II had to say on this matter. So I
looked it up in the constitutions and decrees of the Council itself, as
well as in the liturgical documents and revised Code of Canon Law
that implemented the conciliar directives. I found that Vatican II
provided clear guidance for the celebration of confirmation. What
Vatican II had to say shaped the changes we eventually made in our
parish practice.

Since then, I have had many opportunities to discuss the issue of
when to confirm with parents, fellow pastors and other parish
ministers. In such conversations, people often are surprised that we
have clear directives and an underlying rationale for the celebration of
confirmation—at what age and in what sequence. I have been asked,
"Where can I find what Vatican II says? Which documents? What
paragraph numbers? Which canons in church law give direction for
the celebration of confirmation?"

So I went back and collected the pertinent passages. I offer them here as a parish resource.

The Sacraments of Initiation

1. Baptism, confirmation and first communion are to be understood as initiatory rites, whether celebrated with adults or with children.
2. Confirmation, in particular, must be rethought and reshaped as an initiation rite and be more closely linked to baptism for its meaning and practice.
3. The initiatory sacraments are to be understood and celebrated in the traditional order—baptism, confirmation and first communion—not only with adults, but also with children. This sequence is explained as the liturgical expression of the church's understanding of what God did in the Christ-event and how we come to share in that reality (RCIA, 215). There are no grounds in the reform of Vatican II for deviating from this principle when completing the initiation of children baptized in infancy.
4. There is no difference in the personal readiness required of a candidate for confirmation compared to the readiness required of a first communicant. Readiness for confirmation is even spoken of as the criterion of readiness for first communion. In celebrating initiation sacraments, readiness is relative and varies, depending on the age and condition of the candidate. There is no "objective" readiness, i.e., a specified capacity or level of maturity determined by the meaning of the sacrament.
5. The Latin Rite tradition of a two-step initiation process for Catholic children is preserved: The initiation of children baptized in infancy (step one) is completed by celebrating both confirmation and first communion at about age seven (step two).

When to Celebrate Confirmation

1. The 1918 *Code of Canon Law:* "Although the administration of the sacrament of confirmation should preferably be postponed in the Latin Church until about the seventh year of age, nevertheless it can be conferred before that age if the infant is in danger of death or if its administration seems to the minister justified for good and serious reasons" (788).

   In applying this canon to the life of the church, the Congregation of the Sacraments (1932) continued to allow the practice in Latin countries of confirming as soon as possible after baptism, but urged continued catechesis toward compliance with the later age (seven). But the Congregation cautioned that the later age of confirmation should not be construed as authorizing confirmation after first communion. First communion after confirmation remained the norm.

   The Congregation of the Sacraments later (1934) added that in addition to the danger of death, "there may also be other legitimate reasons for anticipating the seventh year in the administration of this Sacrament, especially when it is foreseen that a Bishop or the priest who has the faculty of administering it will be absent for a long time, or when there is some other necessity or just any serious reason" (Bouscaren, *Canon Law Digest 2,* 187).

   Attempts to delay confirmation beyond age seven, to age ten, for example, were firmly condemned by the Code Commission (1952).

2. The *Constitution on the Sacred Liturgy* (1963) of Vatican II called for the reform of the sacrament of confirmation: "The intimate connection that this sacrament has with the whole of Christian initiation is to be more lucidly set forth" (71). To achieve this reform, the praenotanda of the *Rite of Confirmation* and the pertinent canons of the 1983 *Code of Canon Law* identify confirmation, together with baptism and first communion, as part of Christian initiation.

3. The *Rite of Confirmation* (1971) prescribes that for children who were baptized as infants "the administration of confirmation is generally postponed until about the seventh year" (11). Exception: For pastoral reasons, an episcopal conference can prescribe a later age. (In April 1972, the National Conference of Catholic Bishops [NCCB] decided not to choose a later age for confirmation in the United States but allowed an individual bishop to set a later age in his own diocese.)

4. The 1983 *Code of Canon Law* stresses the importance (an obligation) of those baptized but not confirmed to receive confirmation "at the appropriate time" (890) and determines the appropriate time to be "at about the age of discretion" (891). Exception: A national conference of bishops can determine another age. (In November 1984, the NCCB decided not to determine another age for confirmation in the United States. It was decided to let each diocese independently deal with the question of age.)

5. *Pastoral Care of the Sick: Rites of Anointing and Viaticum* (1972/1983) urges a priest to celebrate the sacraments of initiation with a sick child who is unbaptized, including first communion: "If the child is a proper subject of confirmation, then he/she may receive first communion in accordance with the practice of the church" (48).

Sequence and Unity of Initiatory Rites

1. The Congregation of the Sacraments in 1932 "declared it was truly opportune and even more conformable to the nature and effects of the sacrament of confirmation that children should not approach the sacred table for the first time unless after the reception of the sacrament of confirmation, which is, as it were, the complement of baptism and in which is given the fullness of the Holy Spirit. They did not intend, however, to keep from the sacred table those who heretofore have been admitted when they had reached the age of discretion, even

though they had no opportunity of receiving the sacrament of confirmation previously" (Bouscaren, *Canon Law Digest 1,* 349).

2. In the documents of Vatican II, baptism, confirmation and first communion are identified as the sacraments of Christian initiation. They invariably are described in that sequence and closely linked to each other when celebrated. First communion invariably is located as the completion of full initiation. The following descriptions of the sequence and unity of these sacraments are typical:

   Dogmatic Constitution on the Church (1964): "It is through the sacraments . . . that the nature and organic structure of the priestly community is brought into operation." The faithful are "incorporated into the church through baptism . . . bound more intimately to the church by the sacrament of confirmation . . . take part in the eucharistic sacrifice, the fount and apex of the whole Christian life" (11).

   Decree on the Ministry and Life of Priests (1965): "Hence the eucharist shows itself to be the source and the apex of the whole work of preaching the gospel. . . . The faithful, already marked with the sacred seal of baptism and confirmation, are through the reception of the eucharist fully joined to the body of Christ" (5).

3. *Christian Initiation,* General Introduction (1969): "Through baptism men and women are incorporated into Christ. . . . [They are] signed with the gift of the Spirit in confirmation. . . . Finally they come to the table of the eucharist. . . . Thus the three sacraments of Christian initiation closely combine" (1, 2).

4. The *Rite of Confirmation* (1971), Apostolic Constitution of Paul VI: "The faithful are born anew by baptism, strengthened by the sacrament of confirmation, and finally are sustained by the food of eternal life in the eucharist. . . . The link between confirmation and the other sacraments of initiation is shown forth more clearly not only by closer association of these sacraments but also by the rite and words by which confirmation is

conferred. . . . Confirmation is so closely linked with the holy eucharist that the faithful, after being signed by holy baptism and confirmation, are incorporated fully into the body of Christ by participation in the eucharist."

5. The *Rite of Confirmation:* "Adult catechumens and children who are baptized at an age when they are old enough for catechesis should ordinarily be admitted to confirmation and the eucharist at the same time they receive baptism" (11). "Ordinarily confirmation takes place within Mass in order to express more clearly the fundamental connection of this sacrament with the entirety of Christian initiation. The latter reaches its culmination in the communion of the body and blood of Christ. The newly confirmed should therefore participate in the eucharist which completes their Christian initiation" (13).

6. The *Rite of Christian Initiation of Adults* (1972/1988): "The third step in the Christian initiation of adults is the celebration of the sacraments of baptism, confirmation, and eucharist. Through this final step the elect, receiving pardon for their sins, are admitted into the people of God. They are graced with adoption as children of God and are led by the Holy Spirit into the promised fullness of time begun in Christ and, as they share in the eucharistic sacrifice and meal, even to a foretaste of the kingdom of God" (206). "According to the ancient practice followed in the Roman liturgy, adults are not to be baptized without receiving confirmation immediately afterward, unless some serious reason stands in the way. The conjunction of the two celebrations signifies the unity of the paschal mystery, the close link between the mission of the Son and the outpouring of the Holy Spirit, and the connection between the two sacraments through which the Son and the Holy Spirit come with the Father to those who are baptized" (215).

"Christian Initiation of Children Who Have Reached Catechetical Age" (RCIA, 252–330) envisions two groups of children who are preparing together for Christian initiation:

(1) unbaptized children of catechetical age who are preparing for initiation into the church and (2) a peer group of baptized Catholic children who are preparing to complete their initiation by confirmation and first communion (254). The catechetical instruction of the two groups combined should be scheduled so that, if possible, at Easter the unbaptized children can be fully initiated and the baptized children can receive confirmation and first communion (256), perhaps even at the same liturgy (308, 322, 329). When unbaptized children and baptized children are initiated together, it is imperative that the baptized children be confirmed before they receive their first communion. To achieve this sequence, when a priest presides, the bishop should grant him the faculty to confirm the baptized children (308).

7. National Statutes for the Catechumenate (1986): "The Rite of Reception into the Full Communion of the Catholic Church respects the traditional sequence of confirmation before eucharist. . . . The confirmation of such candidates should not be deferred, nor should they be admitted to the eucharist until they are confirmed" (35).

8. The 1983 *Code of Canon Law*: "The sacraments of baptism, confirmation, and the Most Holy Eucharist are so interrelated that they are required for full Christian initiation" (842).

9. *Pastoral Care of the Sick: Rites of Anointing and Viaticum* (1972/ 1983): "If it is appropriate, the priest may discuss with the parents the possibility of preparing and celebrating with the child the sacraments of initiation (baptism, confirmation, eucharist). The priest may baptize and confirm the child. To complete the process of initiation, the child should also receive first communion. (If the child is a proper subject for confirmation, then he or she may receive first communion in accordance with the practice of the church.) There is no reason to delay this, especially if the illness is likely to be a long one" (48).

Celebration of Passage: Childhood to Adolescence

DAVID M. BEAUDOIN

W HAT DO WE DO when there is no eighth-grade confirmation? How can we, through catechesis and ritual, help children in the eighth grade to understand and celebrate their passage from childhood to adolescence in light of our Catholic faith? When a parish celebrates confirmation as a sacrament of initiation in close proximity to baptism or first eucharist, rather than in the eighth grade (or later), the parish is faced with the pastoral challenge of celebrating the experience of eighth-grade passage.

A variety of pastoral responses is possible as this new situation is experienced in parishes, all with their own unique needs. Such response must be founded and exist within the context of our Catholic catechetical and liturgical traditions.

Catechetical and Liturgical Principles

As pastors and catechists, we are challenged to minister to people in significant times of their lives. We are challenged to share our faith respectful of the integrity of the Christian message and of the dignity of the person.

Virgil Michel, OSB, the founding editor of *Orate Fratres (Worship),* wrote numerous articles concerning liturgy and catechesis. In "Rediscovering the Obvious: Liturgy and the Psychology of Education" (*Orate Fratres* 14 [October 1940]), Michel suggested that a series of pedagogical principles, which were newly discovered by many educational theorists and researchers of his day, "have been part and parcel of the church's traditional method of teaching through liturgy." Michel affirmed these insights as sound pedagogical principles, reflective of traditional liturgical norms, though at the time — the 1920s and 1930s — somewhat forgotten. He proposed that as a creative approach to catechetics, these principles would serve to ground effective religious education. Michel also called for liturgical renewal that reflected this traditional wisdom. The principles are:

1. *Method and materials must be adapted to the capacity of the learner.* According to Michel, this is the "sacramental principle."
2. *Proceed from the concrete to the abstract.* Liturgy employs water, wine, oil, bread, ashes, fire, salt, palms, incense, colors, words and gestures that speak to the senses as "concrete signs that convey their message to the soul in accordance with the natural aptitudes" of the person.
3. *Learning is fostered by doing.* Liturgy calls for active participation through gesturing, talking, listening, singing, reading, praying and intentional participation in the action of the celebration.
4. *Learning is fostered by group process and dialogue.* Liturgy is the collective action of the community that requires participation in its dialogue form of prayer.
5. *Learning is fostered by repetition of the theme.* Liturgy develops a theme through "the frequent use of a keynote statement in various proper parts of the Mass."
6. *Learning involves growth.* According to Michel, "Liturgy is marked by a sense of progressive development and growth in Christ and union with God."

Michel said in conclusion, "Thus the liturgy makes its appeal to the whole person, to the understanding and the senses, to the emotional and aesthetic life and to the will. It furnishes both the basis and the inspiration for constant spiritual growth of the integral person in all the elements of his or her nature." Michel insisted that liturgy and catechesis must respect the integrity of the person. Much of what he wrote concerning catechetical methodology is affirmed by *Sharing the Light of Faith: National Catechetical Directory for Catholics of the United States* (NCD), especially in the chapter titled, "Catechesis toward Maturity in Faith."

These catechetical and liturgical principles serve as solid ground for a creative pastoral response to the eighth grader's experience of passage from childhood to adolescence.

The Child in Eighth Grade

The NCD and *The Challenge of Adolescent Catechesis: Maturing in Faith,* published by the National Federation for Catholic Youth Ministry, provide valuable insights on the catechetical circumstances of pre-adolescent children (ages 10–13) and adolescents. Most children in the eighth grade are around 13 years old. Each child is unique but, because of his or her experience of shared humanity, has some of those qualities that are characteristic of persons their age.

The child in the eighth grade is growing rapidly in his or her capacity for freedom, consciousness, responsibility, knowledge and love. The term "apprenticeship" in Christian living captures the meaning of the circumstances of an eighth-grade child. As an apprentice, the 13-year-old child is capable of much free and responsible activity, reflective thinking, appropriate emotional responses and healthy interpersonal relationships but, as an apprentice, the 13-year-old child needs the guidance of those more experienced and skilled in human activities. The apprentice has not yet fully developed the habits and surefooted patterns of thinking and behaving that ground mature adult development.

The 13-year-old is in transition from the dependency of childhood toward the personal responsibility of adolescence and adulthood.

It is often a tumultuous passage for everyone involved: child, parents, teachers, ministers and friends.

Empirical research concerning the psychology of the eighth-grade child validates the observations and intuitions of parents, teachers and pastors. The 13-year-old is involved in a process of dramatic and rapid change. In particular, the 13-year-old is confronted with physical and emotional changes that go to the core of personal and interpersonal life.

The NCD says:

> Important physical changes have a direct bearing on how preadolescents perceive other people and relate to them. Young people at this stage face the task of coming to terms with themselves and others as sexual beings. While the foundations for doing so are laid in infancy, the effort now becomes conscious. They need to accept themselves precisely as male or female and to acquire a whole new way of relating to others. Usually, too, this involves some confusion, uncertainty, curiosity, awkwardness and experimentation as young people try on different patterns of behavior while searching for their unique identity. Puberty also adds a new dimension to the practice of personal freedom: increased responsibility for directing one's actions, together with increased readiness to accept their consequences. (105)

Peer values, attitudes and behavior play a crucial role in the life of the child. As they develop a greater sense of identity and belonging to their peer group, adolescents seek to maintain a distance from the significant adults in their lives (parents and teachers). Yet because of their struggles with self-doubt, they are often, in an unconscious way, dependent on these adults for their "no strings attached" emotional support and love. They also look for adult role models and affirmation outside the immediacy of the home and school or to older adults such as grandparents. As the 13-year-old child becomes aware of his or her identity and begins to develop a capacity for relationships and friendships, he or she also develops a greater capacity to experience faith as a personal friendship with God in a faith community.

Planning the Process and Ritual

With both Michel's pedagogical/liturgical principles and an under-standing of the state-of-being of the 13-year-old as background, plan-ning catechesis and ritual to mark this passage can begin. A planning team should be formed when a parish acknowledges the need to min-ister to its children who are experiencing the life passage from child-hood to adolescence. The catechetical process employed in a parish should be designed and implemented by people who are sensitive to the particular concerns of the eighth graders in that community. The team should be comprised of people who are skilled in the theory and practice of religious education and liturgy. Nearly every parish has such people; often they are the veteran school and religious education teachers. It also is appropriate to involve parents, parishioners and the children in the planning.

In its efforts to design a catechetical process and prayer ritual, the planning team needs to determine how this process will fit into the parish's total religious education program. The team must deal with practical questions. What should the doctrinal content be? What form should the ritual take? What pedagogical methods should be used? When should the catechesis and ritual occur? How will the process relate to the eighth-grade religion curriculum and to eighth-grade graduation? Who should be involved in the process and ritual? These questions should be addressed in a way that is consistent with catechetical and liturgical norms.

Two documents from the National Conference of Catholic Bishops—*To Teach as Jesus Did* and *Basic Teachings for Catholic Religious Education*—provide catechetical norms. *To Teach as Jesus Did* speaks of three interlocking dimensions of the integrated educational mission of the church: "the message revealed by God *(didache)* that the church proclaims; fellowship in the life of the Holy Spirit *(koinonia),* service to the Christian community and the entire human community *(diako-nia)*" (3–4). The bishops state, "Educational programs for the young must strive to teach doctrine, to do so within the experience of Christian community, and to prepare individuals for effective Chris-tian witness and service to others" (22).

In *Basic Teachings for Catholic Religious Education,* the bishops propose that there are three themes that carry through all religious education: the importance of prayer; participating in liturgy; familiarity with the Holy Bible (3–4). In terms of methodology, NCD maintains that the message must be faithfully presented according to the circumstances and ability of those being catechized. Later in *Basic Teachings,* the value of both a deductive and inductive approach is affirmed; however:

> The deductive approach provides its fullest impact when preceded by the inductive. . . . Experiential learning, which can be considered a form of inductive methodology, gives rise to concerns and questions, hopes and anxieties, reflections and judgments that increase one's desire to penetrate deeply into life's meaning. Experience can also increase the intelligibility of the Christian message by providing illustrations and examples which shed light on the truths of revelation. At the same time, experience itself should be interpreted in the light of revelation. (101)

Catechists are invited to encourage people to "reflect on their significant experiences and respond to God's presence there. They should seek to reach the whole person, using both cognitive (intellectual) and affective (emotional) techniques."

The pastoral challenge is to design and implement a program that focuses on the relationship between the life experience of eighth-grade passage and those specific aspects of the Christian message that can shed light on this pivotal human experience. The catechetical goal of this reflection on human experience in light of revelation is a better understanding and living of the Christian life.

The *Directory for Masses with Children* (Sacred Congregation for Divine Worship, 1973) and the NCD (in "Catechesis for a Worshiping Community") provide insights that ought to be considered in planning and celebrating a ritual for eighth-grade passage. The planning team makes decisions about the ritual and its relation to the liturgy. The NCD provides helpful insights on the connections between catechesis, liturgy and human experience. It says:

> As for catechesis, it prepares people for full and active participation in
> liturgy (by helping them understand its nature, rituals and symbols) and
> at the same time flows from liturgy, inasmuch as, reflecting upon the
> community's experiences of worship, it seeks to relate them to daily life
> and to growth in faith. (66)

The symbols used to celebrate the ritual of passage ought to reflect the human experience of passage and move people to affirm God's creative and saving presence in this experience. Virgil Michel's liturgical insights serve as valuable tools for designing the ritual. Developing prayer rituals requires a particular sensitivity to sound liturgical theory and practice. Creative experimentation takes place in dialogue with the Catholic liturgical tradition.

This human experience of passage from childhood to adolescence holds the seeds of a greater understanding of Christian hope for participation in the death and new life of Jesus Christ. Catechesis invites a person to reflect on the human experience and to respond affirmatively to God's grace which is offered there. As the person moves from childhood to adolescence, he or she is invited to grow in faith. Catechesis challenges the eighth-grade child to become a new creation in Christ in the midst of a fleshy experience of becoming new.

Lent appears to be a suitable time for the implementation of the catechetical process because of the lenten focus on life, death, passover. The ritual could be celebrated during the Easter season. Scriptural texts that tell stories or speak of passage, new life, new creation, change and resurrection serve as the message or "content" of the process. Parents, sponsors, parishioners and friends join teachers, parish ministers and children-in-passage for the process and ritual. The eighth-grade children give service to other people-in-passage. A planning team arranges to incorporate the eighth graders into the celebrations of anointing of the sick, baptism, marriage, funerals and first communion. Other people-in-passage may be invited to share their stories. A man and woman preparing for marriage may be invited to share their experience of passage with a particular sensitivity to the eighth-grade person's developing sexuality and interest in interpersonal relationships. A grandparent or widow may come to share wisdom gained in an experience of passage.

There are many creative possibilities. The feelings connected with passage—like fear, disappointment, surprise, anxiety, apprehension, anticipation and happiness—must be respected and understood as an integral part of the human experience in which God is revealed.

We as Christians are invited to recognize and celebrate the saving and creative presence of God in the midst of our changing world and at the core of our many passages. When we do this with eighth graders, we address a specific need and offer these children a vision that will prepare them to be faithful witnesses of God's creative love and saving promise of new life.

Bar Mitzvah: A Modern Perspective on Judaism's Rite of Passage

DEBORAH LEVINE

"TODAY I AM A MAN" has become synonymous with bar mitzvah, the Jewish ritual marking the passage from boyhood into the adult life of the congregation. Perhaps no other Jewish life-cycle event, with the possible exception of the *brith* (circumcision), symbolizes so well Jewish tradition and community. But the place of the bar mitzvah in Jewish life is changing as is the emphasis on this phrase and on the ritual. As a Jewish woman active in the Jewish community, my interest in these changes in the performance, the perception and the (once exclusively masculine) nature of this rite, is both intellectual and personal.

The religious meaning of the event is evident in the name itself. "Bar mitzvah" in English is literally "the son of commandment," one who is "duty bound." The rite marks a boy's assumption of the responsibilities, obligations and traditions of the Jewish community. The ritual ceremony generally, though not always, takes place on the first Sabbath after the completion of the 13th year of a boy's life.

Origins and Meaning

The origin of the bar mitzvah is not well documented, but it would appear that the ceremony, as we know it, was established in fourteenth-century Germany. While there are earlier references in Jewish litera-ture and oral tradition implying maturity of boys after their 13th year (12th year for girls), it is not clear how passage into adulthood was marked prior to this date. The bar mitzvah, when it began, celebrated the changed status; it did not confer it. Adulthood was conferred on girls with no celebration of the event.

The bar mitzvah marked and continues to mark certain legal and religious aspects of the boy's life, law and religion being intertwined in Jewish tradition. He now may form part of the *minyan,* the ten men necessary for a prayer service; he is required to observe the fast days such as Yom Kippur; he is liable for his own misdeeds; he has the ability to make vows and to buy and sell property; and eventually he can serve on the *bet din* (the legal/religious court). As an adult, he assumes all the obligations of ritual on holidays and synagogue participation.

The interaction of father and son is symbolic of this passing into manhood. The father prays over the boy, giving a paternal blessing. He also thanks God for relieving him of the duty of caring for the son because the boy has become a man and is responsible for his own deeds. The young man is called to speak in front of the congregation for the first time, usually to read from the Torah (and later, perhaps, to give a learned discourse with a Jewish theme). The father, grandfather or other male relatives join the boy on the *bimah* (podium) during the prayer service to mark this passing from childhood into the ranks of the adults.

Typically, a young man in the early European ghetto would prepare for his bar mitzvah by studying prescribed prayers, Torah, the commentaries on the Torah that make up the oral tradition of Judaism and Hebrew, the language of religious discourse. He would be instructed in the use of the prayer shawl, head covering and phylac-teries, boxes of prayers bound on the hands and forehead. All male adults used phylacteries, which became symbolic of the bar mitzvah.

The exclusively masculine nature of the bar mitzvah should be stressed. The *minyan, bet din* and other legal/religious responsibilities revolving around the synagogue and Torah were enjoyed only by males. In ghetto life and in many traditional communities today, women's presence in the synagogue was not required. Women were not permitted to read from the Torah, particularly in the context of a synagogue service. Women's religious responsibilities centered on the home. Modern traditional women retain much of this division, but the role of women in Jewish religious life has been one of the major points of debate in modern times.

Movements for Reform

An example of this debate can be seen as early as 1810 in Germany where attempts were made to adapt the bar mitzvah rite by creating a rite for both boys and girls. This new rite was modeled after Christian practices and was called confirmation. This attempt signaled the beginning of a reform movement within Judaism.

The push for reform intensified when large numbers of Jews immigrated to America. In this country, Jews had no need or even possibility of maintaining the way of life of the European ghetto. Geographic dispersal and the lack of religious and legal restrictions on Jews brought a reform of many traditional practices. These changes were institutionalized in different branches of Judaism: Reform, Conservative and Reconstructionist. Even among those who prefer to be called Orthodox Jews, a considerable variety of opinions on traditional observances and law developed.

The struggle to redefine a rite of passage also led to the adaptation of bar mitzvah for women in Italy and France during the nineteenth century. Called bat mitzvah or "daughter of commandment," the adaptation originally did not include the reading from the Torah, nor was the ceremony necessarily performed in the synagogue. The bat mitzvah had very limited popularity until emigration to this country. Judas Kaplan Eisenstein brought it to New York in 1922.

Ironically, while encouraging the participation of women in Torah services, the Reform Movement in its most classical form downplayed the importance of the bat mitzvah. The Hebrew necessary for the bar/bat mitzvah frequently was deleted from the Jewish education curriculum in American synagogues. In contrast, confirmation became increasingly popular among Reform Jews.

In the nineteenth century, confirmation originally was performed on the same Sabbath as a boy's bar mitzvah and complemented the ceremony. At its inception, the rite was not observed in the synagogue, nor was it welcomed there by many traditionalists. However, confirmation spread to progressive congregations in Germany, France, Denmark and the United States.

Confirmation in American was placed at Shavuot, one of the three major harvest/pilgrimage holidays. Shavuot also commemorates God's gift of the Ten Commandments and Israel's acceptance of them. It is this link to the commandments that was chosen for confirmation, echoing the bar mitzvah. The age of confirmation was raised to the midteens to provide additional Jewish education beyond bar mitzvah, an important issue for a community whose children would attend secular public schools.

Confirmation now is observed in the synagogue, but no longer is celebrated on an individual basis. An entire class is confirmed at once, after demonstrating their knowledge of Judaism. The ceremony includes music, a procession, a prayer and sermon by the rabbi emphasizing the community's renewal of the covenant with God.

Women, as well as men, now can have a bat mitzvah or a confirmation or both. They learn Hebrew and the prayers in the worship service liturgy. Women now may wear the traditional prayer shawl, phylacteries and yarmulke, read from the Torah and be part of a *minyan* in Reform, Reconstructionist and liberal Conservative congregations.

Contemporary Practice and Debate

Preparation for a bar or bat mitzvah participant mirrors the changing times in nontraditional congregations. The young adult frequently will give a variation on a speech that is written by teachers and tutors rather than a learned discourse. The use of the ancient chants for the Hebrew in the Torah reading is not so widespread as it once was. The study of the Talmud is limited. While a certain degree of Hebrew knowledge will be demonstrated, the ritual sometimes marks the end of Jewish studies rather than the beginning of serious membership in the scholarly community. Some families dispense with the rite altogether, while others concentrate on giving a large party following the synagogue ceremony. The variety of responses in large part may correspond to the blurred relationship of the bar/bat mitzvah and synagogue life.

Many professionals are urging the return of some traditional practices in the prayer service to regain a sense of the religious importance of such rites as the bar mitzvah. Rabbis now graduating from Reform and Reconstructionist Jewish seminaries incorporate many elements of tradition that once were discarded by classical Reform Judaism. Conservative congregations have maintained many traditional practices but these vary considerably.

In this country, most congregations have a varied membership. Differences in background and orientation are reflected in the decisions made for bar/bat mitzvahs. While background may dictate the same for confirmation, this ritual is a group exercise with less room for individuality. It is through an analysis of the bar/bat mitzvah that one can see how the choices made on the basis of background actually affect members of the congregation. The individualized nature of the rite prompts examination on a personal level within its historical context. For this more personal analysis, one must go beyond this historical and religious explanation and look at particular cases.

The Experience of My Family

My own family can be used as an example of varying experiences of bar/bat mitzvah and, to some degree, confirmation. While there is no typical family, my family's experiences with bar/bat mitzvah is not unusual in the Jewish community. My father came from an Orthodox Jewish background and his bar mitzvah was performed in a very traditional service. My mother came from a family that had lived in Bermuda since the turn of the century where Jewish tradition, education and communal life were difficult to pursue.

One of the primary reasons my parents immigrated to the United States from Bermuda was to enable their children to receive a Jewish education. My older brother Joseph was old enough to start preparation for bar mitzvah and it was important to them that he would be able to do so. They made the choice of a Conservative synagogue for Joe's study and bar mitzvah. The emphasis on tradition in this congregation was similar to what my father had experienced as a young man.

Joe, who had been used to living among non-Jews and had little concept and familiarity with Jewish tradition, must have experienced considerable culture shock. He now owned phylacteries and other apparel for prayer and worship. He had to learn Hebrew quickly and with enough mastery to have a bar mitzvah in only a year or so. He had to participate in prayer services unavailable in Bermuda with a liturgy he rarely had used.

While Joe would take enormous pride in the achievements connected with his bar mitzvah, I think the family found the rite more meaningful than he did. To the family, relatives and friends, Joe's bar mitzvah was a renewal of their commitment to Judaism and a celebration of family. After his bar mitzvah, Joe dropped his pursuit of a Jewish education. However, he renewed his interest in Judaism when the time came for his own son's bar mitzvah. Regardless of any ambivalence that he felt about his own experience, he stood behind his son on the *bimah,* recited the blessings and draped the prayer shawl over his son's shoulders. The strength of tradition and the bar mitzvah is undeniable.

Shortly after Joe's bar mitzvah, my mother took a job teaching in the religious school of a Reform Congregation. She had virtually no background in Jewish studies and had to learn on the job. She took me along as her assistant. Together, we struggled to keep ahead of the children. My mother attended Hebrew Union College and earned not only a teacher's certificate, but a principal's license. She learned Hebrew, tutored children for their bar/bat mitzvah and became principal of one of the largest religious schools in the Midwest. She had neither a bat mitzvah nor confirmation.

My younger brother Jonathan had an entirely different experience. Jon's bar mitzvah was performed in a Reform synagogue. There was no need to learn how to wear the phylacteries. The prayer shawl draped on him at the ceremony never was intended for much use because none of the men in the congregation wore one. The same applied to the *yarmulke* (skullcap) that he wore for the occasion. However, he had gone through religious school and was familiar with the synagogue, the service and the Torah in a way that Joe was not.

Jon's experience differed from his older brother's in another way. Jon had special needs because of a significant learning disability problem. As difficult as it had been to learn to read and write English, it was all the more difficult to learn Hebrew. Reading biblical Hebrew can be particularly problematic with a learning disability because the writing is usually small, contains no vowels and includes some unusual grammatical constructions not found in modern-day Hebrew.

There are many children like Jon who might not seek a bar mitzvah. Nor would their families actively pursue such a goal for fear of failure and embarrassment. It was because my mother insisted that the training be adapted for people with learning disabilities that Jon had a bar mitzvah. She developed a method for teaching him that she applied to other learning-disabled children and, later, to children with problems ranging from drugs to emotional disturbances. Her success with these children demonstrates that the bar/bat mitzvah offers invaluable benefits for this often-ignored population.

There is little doubt that this group of children benefited from the bar/bat mitzvah process more than any other group in the synagogue. These children experience great difficulties blending into the mainstream of any social group. The bar/bat mitzvah gives them a chance to aim for concrete goals with discreet tasks and a chance to gain recognition and admiration. They see their efforts bringing joy to some parents, relatives, friends and community. While some teachers claim that at least 70 percent of bar/bat mitzvah participants experience a heightened sense of maturation while preparing for the rite, the percentage among disabled children appears to be much higher.

My own experience illustrates some of the basic problems arising from the unevenness of the Reform Movement. Although bat mitzvah was practiced when we came to this country, I did not participate in this rite. At the time, we could not afford to pay for the extra Hebrew lessons and the specific preparation that was needed. My parents decided that it was more important for my brothers to have a bar mitzvah. Neither religious law nor the then-prevailing community opinion was such that a bat mitzvah was required for me.

I was not permitted on the *bimah* at my younger brother's bar mitzvah. When my father requested that I fill in for my great uncle so that he, my father, would not be the only relative representing the male side of the family, the rabbi denied his request. He said that I could not be called to the Torah without my having had a bat mitzvah. Though I had been confirmed, I felt barred from participation in synagogue life.

My confirmation itself was quite memorable. All the members of my tenth-grade class were all confirmed together, with a large formal procession, inspiring music and sermon. Yet, I did not have a sense of celebrating an adult status in which I received new obligations and privileges. More meaningful to me was my graduation from the religious high school two years after confirmation. This was highly individualized and required a presentation by each of us to the congregation. These extra years of study and reflection and the personal effort they required meant more to me than all the previous years of religious schooling.

Neither confirmation nor graduation nor my years on the staff of the American Jewish Committee have allayed the feeling of loss from not having a bat mitzvah. It is a situation that I fully intend to correct. One of the more interesting by-products of the Reform Movement is that bar/bat mitzvah can take place at any age after 13. Adults can and do avail themselves of the opportunity to have a bar/bat mitzvah. Many women who have gotten caught in the changing trends have taken that opportunity.

My daughter, Roslyn, will approach her bat mitzvah as a natural course of events. She has been learning Hebrew since the primary grades. She assumes that I will be on the *bimah* with her when the time comes. And like any other preteen, she already is thinking of the styles and colors of the prayer shawl that she will receive. I bought myself a prayer shawl at the age of 40 and didn't have a clue as to what to do with it. I am both envious and grateful that she will be at ease with it.

My emotional attachment to the bar/bat mitzvah is in part because of its having been unattainable. The lure of a hard-won achievement is irresistible especially in an area where access has been denied. There is a continual sense of having unfinished business, of needing the experiences of standing before the congregation, reading from the Torah and using the ancient chants. This need goes beyond any logical analysis and is a testimony to the power of a rite rooted in tradition and the community fabric.

Does the Bar/Bat Mitzvah Have a Future?

Not everyone in the Jewish community agrees that the bar/bat mitzvah has value in modern times. Several parents have voiced their skepticism to me about the importance of the event in their children's lives. A few people expressed ambivalence about their daughters participating in some of the traditionally male aspects of bar mitzvah, such as wearing the prayer shawl. One or two parents felt that most of their congregation was indifferent to the rite and that their rabbis showed only moderate interest in its performance.

In general, however, most Jews affirm the importance of the bar/ bat mitzvah. The rabbi of a small suburban Chicago congregation, Stephen Bob, notes that the bar/bat mitzvah always will retain importance as a sacred rite for sons and daughters while confirmation will continue to mark educational achievement, but not have the status of a life-cycle event.

Herman Schaalman, rabbi emeritus of a large Chicago synagogue, noted:

> The stress of our mobile society on adolescence makes the bar/bat
> mitzvah more important than ever. The ritual emphasizes and
> encourages the development of values and commitment for young
> people in a community that no longer automatically serves this
> function. The growing acceptance of bat mitzvah for women of all ages

also serves to bring into the community those who have the needed talents and energies but who have felt disenfranchised.

The very personal and hard-won achievement of the bar/bat mitzvah makes the experience a deeply moving, integrative force in the Jewish community. My mother's description of Bert, one of her disabled students celebrating his bar mitzvah, illustrates the impact on the participant, family and congregation and conveys the spiritual dimension of the event:

> It was frankly an emotional experience for all, with everyone happy and proud. Happiest and proudest was Bert himself. After the ceremony he told me, "This is the best day of my life. I wish it would last forever." Anyone looking at his glowing face had to rejoice with him.

Rite of Christian Initiation of Adults: Some Pastoral Implications for Teens

JAMES A. WILDE

O N THE SOLEMNITY of Epiphany, 1972, some wonderful, long-hidden contours of the paschal mystery were disclosed, a key result of Vatican II. The *Ordo initiationis christianae adultorum (Order of Christian Initiation of Adults),* the first word of which was rendered *Rite* by the International Committee on English in the Liturgy (ICEL) in their 1974 translation (hereafter, RCIA), was promulgated by the Vatican.

Teens gain several things from the RCIA: (1) an order of Christian initation for teen adults; (2) an order of Christian initiation for teen children; (3) a coherent vision of God, creation and the church—the dimensions of which even most adults do not yet have—for *all* teens: whether they never have been baptized, whether they were baptized but never catechized, whether they were baptized and fully catechized or whether they were baptized and catechized and now are candidates for full communion in another tradition. Without this vision—the necessary context for Christian initiation and for Christian life—

Christianity in the twentieth and twenty-first centuries makes little sense for teens or anyone else.

Whether the teens were initiated into Christianity earlier in life or just now are considering it, whether they are adults or children, whether they have found meaning for life or still are searching, the RCIA has something for them.

Christian Initiation of Teen Adults

Without doubt, some teens qualify legally, chronologically, academically, emotionally, socially and spiritually as adults. They may be fully competent to marry on their own authority. They may vote responsibly. They may serve in the military or be conscientious objectors. They may distinguish themselves as authentic workers for justice and peace. They may be able legally to stand trial as adults. And they may have the personal resources either to disown or to own for themselves the faith of Christians. When such teens inquire into Christianity, RCIA, 1–251 applies to them.

FRUITFUL DISCERNMENT

As individual teen adults and the local church discern themselves ready for each other, the RCIA follows. The critical two-way discernment with all adults and with any Christian community takes on no less importance when the adults are teens. An affirmative discernment says that the teen adults consider this particular Christian community able to meet their ecclesial needs, e.g., for tradition, authentic worship, apostolic work, hospitality, evangelization, faithfulness to the biblical Christ. It says that this community can recognize Christ in these teen adults and will listen to the voice of God as that voice resonates through them.

A reciprocal strengthening of faith happens between a Christian community whose members represent all ages and an adult teen. The vision of a young adult can work wonders in a Christian community that opens itself to the presence of the Holy Spirit in that person. A younger member of a catechumenal faith-sharing group has a responsibility and a perspective that older members may highly value. Such appreciation may come as well from older members of the larger Christian community. And the discovery of a grateful, affirming community of faith can enhance a young adult's life with God and encourage a commitment to social justice and peace.

CAUTION

Teen adults are not yet settled in a career, frequently not yet finished with their education and often not committed to their life's main form of service: marriage, family, ordained ministry, religious life or single life. Sometimes major decisions in these areas are being made simultaneously with the decision about whether or not to be a Christian. Catechumenal team members, instructors and youth ministers must be careful about these special circumstances.

In practice, what an awareness of this massive decision-making time means for ministers is: Never apply external pressure on teen adults to decide quickly. This advice counters that given in a workshop on how to close sales. This wisdom also contradicts the example of cults that take advantage of youth's idealism and disillusionment through brainwashing, propaganda, pressure, half-truths, recruitment strategies, scare tactics. Christianity is for free adults with a long view. It is not a quick fix for personal and social ills.

ACCOMPANYING AN ADULT TEEN ON THE JOURNEY OF FAITH

This special care on the part of the pastoral team regarding adult teens is required even more on the part of sponsors and godparents. Being present to an adult teen through inquiry, acceptance into the order of catechumens, the catechumenate, election or enrollment of names, purification and enlightenment, the sacraments of initiation, mystagogy and beyond demands empathy, respect, integrity and, most of all, an openness to the same journey for oneself. The teen adult needs a faithful companion for the journey.

Two qualities of special importance in companioning a teen adult are a life of public and private prayer and a life of commitment to community building and peacemaking. These qualities comprise "Adult Christianity 101." Without them, Christianity is merely a game. With them, the journey has a beginning, a direction and a goal. It is a journey of faith, ongoing conversion, with Christ as the beginning and end.

Adult teens easily can spot the phoniness when these qualities are absent. It would be tragic to misguide a young adult into thinking that a Christian actually can get along without a life of prayer or that social apathy is acceptable in a Christian.

Individual and group wrestling with the biblical texts of the Sunday liturgy of the word during the process of Christian initiation is the surest and richest resource for this life of prayer and social commitment. The Sunday-by-Sunday catechumenal rite of dismissal and formal lectionary-based catechesis can create in the catechumen a hunger for eucharist, a desire to pray and a thirst for justice and peace. For many adult teens, this approach can prove fruitful. The RCIA would have the word of God and the prayer of the church lead these teens in spirit and in truth.

Christian Initiation of Teen Children

According to RCIA, 252, the first chapter of Part II, "Christian Initiation of Children Who Have Reached Catechetical Age," is intended for children not baptized as infants, who have attained the use of reason and are of catechetical age. They seek Christian initiation either at the direction of their parents or guardians or, with parental permission, on their own initiative. Such children are capable of receiving and nurturing a personal faith and of recognizing an obligation in conscience. They cannot yet be treated as adults because, at this stage of their lives, they are dependent on their parents or guardians and still are strongly influenced by their companions and their social surroundings. At present, a helpful resource for this ministry is *Issues in the Christian Initiation of Children: Catechesis and Liturgy,* edited by Kathy Brown and Frank Sokol (Chicago: Liturgy Training Publications, 1989).

Terms such as "catechetical age," "adult catechesis," "adult" and "child" receive various interpretations. Most commentators on the RCIA include persons from seven or eight to 17 or 18 as "children who have reached catechetical age." The counterpart to "children who have reached catechetical age" in Germany is *Kinder im Schulalter* ("children of school age") and in France is *les enfants et les adolescents en age de scolarité* ("children and adolescents of school age"). *Sharing the Light of Faith: National Catechetical Directory for Catholics of the United States* (Washington: United States Catholic Conference, 1979) freely uses the term "adult catechesis" (9, 32, 40, 46, 117, 185, 188, 192–6). The RCIA also describes the catechesis of adults (75–80, 139, 244–51). On the other side of the age scale, *Sharing the Light of Faith* discusses catechesis for infancy, early childhood, family and preschool children (177, 226, 230). The authors of *Sharing the Light of Faith* assume that even infants can be of catechetical age. These facts point up the ambiguity of the term "catechetical age" as it is used in the RCIA. The statement that this form of the rite is for unbaptized children "who have attained the use of reason" (RCIA, 252) clarifies the term somewhat. In *Sharing the Light of Faith,* every age is catechetical, but the attainment of the use of reason is usually said to occur around the age of seven or eight.

Human Relationships

It is unfair to group teen children *too closely or too consistently* with younger children or with adults. With regard to age, the healthiest initiatory structure for teen children is one that affirms their relationship with a cross section of all of society and at the same time respects their right to some privacy and identity with peers. They need solid human relationships that are one on one, with peers, with peers and younger children, with peers and older children, with the whole Christian assembly and with groups and movements beyond church that represent the whole world. For example, what a tragedy it would be to deprive teen children and elderly persons of each other's company! What a loss to deprive teen children access to the company of young men and women who are preparing for marriage!

In the various rites, catechetical sessions, social events, interviews and ministerial functions that mark the initiatory journey, a variety of settings should be provided for teen children. They must have their age-appropriate gatherings, but they also need expansion room.

THE "CATECHETICAL GROUP"

At least seven times in the text (RCIA, 257, 269, 293 twice, 308, 322, 328), the term "catechetical group" describes a gathering of unbaptized children with already-baptized children of the same age who are latter preparing for confirmation and eucharist or for confirmation only. See also RCIA, 254.1, in which children to be initiated are seen as progressing "gradually and within the supportive setting of this group of companions." Such catechetical groups of unbaptized and baptized children may become more and more familiar in parishes and clusters of Christian communities. The "catechetical group" of this kind is a movement in the direction of accommodating people of similar age but of greater diversity in sacramental, spiritual and catechetical development. Such groups are practical and reasonable answers to some logistical and ministerial questions.

The National Statutes for the Catechumenate (NSC) states the issue clearly:

> Some elements of the ordinary catechetical instruction of baptized children before their reception of the sacraments of confirmation and eucharist may be appropriately shared with catechumens of catechetical age. Their condition and status as catechumens, however, should not be compromised or confused, nor should they receive the sacraments of initiation in any sequence other than that determined in the ritual of Christian initiation. (NSC, 19)

PATIENCE WITH THE RITES, TEEN CHILDREN AND ONESELF

Because the RCIA is new, adult ministers of Christian initiation for children are beginners, and beginners need patience. They should be patient most of all with themselves. The task is marvelous, and they should not expect too much of themselves as leaders these first times around. Mistakes are inevitable, and everyone must be forgiving and start again. Everyone journeys a path that requires courage.

Adult ministers also must be patient with the teen children. Their questions often are uncomfortable—even unanswerable. Openness to the Holy Spirit of Jesus Christ in them can result in many little deaths for the adults. But those same children can lead adults to new life. A patronizing or condescending attitude is inappropriate in Christian ministry.

One way to be patient with the rite is to realize how still young and developing it is. Another way to be patient is not to lose nerve in view of the two different and conflicting ways of initiating children in current practice. Openness and courage may allow contradictions in practice to become even more glaring, but it is hoped that the best options and alternatives will result eventually. The care and respect with which rites are prepared and celebrated can accomplish much with all members of the catechetical group—the baptized as well as the unbaptized—and with members of the assembly. It can touch even outsiders.

SACRAMENTAL CATECHESIS IS NOT RELIGIOUS EDUCATION

Christian initiation of teen children begins a journey of faith in which sacramental catechesis temporarily takes a higher place than religious education. In this initiatory mode, the two primary catechetical functions are the breaking open of the word of God and the breaking open of the sacramental actions.

For teen children to break open the word of God most effectively, the Sunday catechesis of the church after the celebration of the liturgy of the word and the rite of dismissal (RCIA, 276) follows the same order used for adults. Occasionally but not ordinarily, if the circumstances are right, it may be beneficial for young teen catechumens and adult catechumens in a parish to break open the word of God together. Certainly this age mixture can occur fruitfully in a catechumenal family. Sharing the word of God can flourish also among teen children and younger children. More frequently, breaking open the word of God happens best when young teen catechumens are in a group by themselves with a competent catechist.

Breaking open the sacramental actions and symbols of Christian initiation happens best when the liturgical rites themselves set the agenda. These are the symbols of faith that give us identity. They are our teacher. The assembly teaches us. The word teaches us. The cross teaches us. The water teaches us. The white garment teaches us. The laying on of hands teaches us. The oil teaches us. The breaking of the bread teaches us. Drinking from the cup teaches us.

First we experience the action or symbol. Then we express what we experienced. There is no absence of dogmas in such articulation. That is sacramental catechesis. The experiences are the same, but the articulations are different for children, teens and adults. (See RCIA, 75.)

Religious education continues where sacramental catechesis (catechumenal and mystagogical) leaves off. It focuses more on the articulation of the experience than it does on the experience itself and therefore may be subject to cognitive measurement.

BAPTISM, CONFIRMATION, EUCHARIST

When teen children are baptized, they also are confirmed and celebrate first baptismal eucharist on the same occasion. Christian initiation is a long process with one culminating event—not three:

> In order to signify clearly the interrelation or coalescence of the three sacraments which are required for full Christian initiation (*Code of Canon Law* 842, 2), adult candidates, including children of catechetical age, are to receive baptism, confirmation and eucharist in a single eucharistic celebration, whether at the Easter Vigil or, if necessary, at some other time. (NSC, 14)

Furthermore, these teen children are treated by the *Code of Canon Law* and by the RCIA as adults:

> Since children who have reached the use of reason are considered, for purposes of Christian initiation, to be adults (canon 852, 1), their formation should follow the general pattern of the ordinary catechumenate as far as possible, with the appropriate adaptations permitted by the ritual. They should receive the sacraments of baptism, confirmation and eucharist at the Easter Vigil, together with the older catechumens. (NSC, 18)

In dioceses where there still are two patterns of Christian initiation, that is, where individuals baptized in infancy are not confirmed until a later age and where school-age children are initiated according to the norms of the RCIA, for the latter the integrity and unity of the three sacraments of initiation is to be maintained by not delaying confirmation or eucharist. (See RCIA, 215 and 256.) To delay the celebration of confirmation and first baptismal eucharist of teen neophytes to coincide with the confirmation of their peers would be contrary to the norms of the RCIA and the National Statutes. Because the RCIA consistently models the unity of baptism, confirmation and eucharist, if there is to be any delay, all three should be delayed as one. Ordinarily, for the Christian initiation of teen children, baptism, confirmation and eucharist should *not* be separated or celebrated in any other order.

A Vision of God, Creation and Church for All Teens

The RCIA flows directly from sacred scripture, the riches of the patristic tradition and Vatican II. It offers a still-flawed but nevertheless mature picture of Christian sacramental community life. Parents, teachers, pastors, liturgists and other ministers have as much to discover about this picture as teens do. Because unbaptized and baptized teens can affect each other so powerfully within the cate-chetical group, the vision of God, creation and the church might optimally be highly contagious. How much, for example, might I grasp of the tremendous distance between the Spirit of God and the spirit of evil when one of my best teen friends passes through a well-prepared and well-celebrated rite of scrutiny! How much encourage-ment in faith might I receive as a member of the assembly when I see a teen celebrate baptism, confirmation and eucharist at the Paschal Vigil!

GOD'S REIGN IS PRESENT IN CHRIST

The Sunday celebration of the liturgy of the word and the formal lectionary-based catechesis that takes place after the rite of dismissal of the catechumens (RCIA, 67, 75) leads powerfully to this dimension of the vision. The presentations of the creed and the Lord's Prayer (RCIA, 141–6, 157–62, 178–83) as well as the scrutinies and exorcisms (RCIA, 147–9, 150–6, 164–77) lead to this same deep sense of God's reign already present but not yet fully. The whole Christian assembly, especially the members of catechetical groups in which some unbaptized teens are experiencing Christian initiation, learns about God's reign from these words and actions.

Windows to God as Creator, Shepherd, Love, Life, Light, Truth, One, All, Holy, Rock, Shield, Protector, Horizon, Mercy, Ground in Jesus Christ open through celebrations of the word and the scrutinies. God as intimate and God as beyond, God within and God without, God as delightful and God as terrible is revealed through the creed, human beings and all of creation. God as known and God as unknowable invites and entices people on the way of faith in this fascinating yet awesome mystery.

CREATION IS HOLY

The great and small mysteries of the universe disclose God's creative work—in the beginning and continuing today. In the reading about creation (Genesis 1:1—2:3) at the Easter Vigil, the refrain, "God saw how good it was," comes to a climax in the words, "God saw everything that had been made, and behold, it was very good." Likewise, the prayer over the water at the Easter Vigil includes the words, "At the very dawn of creation your Spirit breathed on the waters, making them the wellspring of all holiness" (RCIA, 222).

Teens today must hear about the holiness and goodness of creation. They need help in naming both the goodness and the evil they experience. Their own struggle for health and integrity, their self-doubts, their insight into the delicately balanced ecosystems of nature that far surpasses the insight of their parents at that age, the rapidly communicated news of war and betrayal, the threat of nuclear disaster, drugs and disease—all this must be placed in the perspective of creation, sin and salvation. They must know that Christians believe that death is not the last word. And the RCIA affords ample opportunity for this good news to be proclaimed and integrated.

FAITH OF THE CHURCH

Between the mystery of God and the mystery of creation, bridging and binding them together, comes the faithful prayer of the church, that is, worship on the part of the body of Christ. Liturgy and catechesis give birth to the creed: those lofty yet inadequate words that voice the deepest longings and darkest doubts of the Christian community.

This corporate identity of members within a group is perhaps better modeled than learned by teens. It is *adults* who can learn from *them* about belonging to a group. One does not hear much about peer groups of 30-, 40- or 50-year-old men and women, but one can discover much from teens about the kind of identity such groups offer.

Faithfulness to each other and solidarity within the Christian community—be it household church, peer church, parish church or the church of earth—can be learned *by* everyone *from* everyone. Only Christ has fully integrated this faithfulness and solidarity. Everyone else is on the way.

ONGOING CONVERSION

On the Fifth Sunday in Ordinary Time in Year C, catechumens learn in the lectionary passage from Luke 5:1–11 that Simon Peter recognized Jesus not in the midst of the assembly as Jesus preached to the multitude from the boat near the shore, but alone with Jesus out in the deep, on the high seas, far from the crowd. Conversion may be helped greatly by the example, guidance and prayer of others, but it is largely a task of taking responsibility for oneself.

Furthermore, according to RCIA, 4–8, 42, 75–6, 139, 244–51, conversion is not a once-for-all event. It continues. The Christian is a pilgrim on a restless journey of faith that ends only with arrival at the destination: union with God and God's people in the fullness of the heavenly reign.

Most important, ongoing conversion is a response to God's personal and universal call to holiness. Jesus proclaimed the good news of God: "This is the time of fulfillment. The reign of God is at hand! Reform your lives and believe in the gospel" (Mark 1:15). "Now God calls on all people everywhere to reform their lives" (Acts 17:31). "Do you not know that God's kindness is an invitation for you to reform" (Romans 2:4).

THE JOURNEY IS PASCHAL

From death to life, from slavery to freedom, from sleep to waking, from night to day, from sin to grace, from part to whole, from I to we, from war to peace, from disease to health, from foolishness to wisdom, from many to one—the journey of the Christian is the paschal journey of Christ. It is passover. It is passing always through death and always to life. This is the meaning of the cross. At the Easter Vigil, the invitation to the promises of baptism are "Dear friends, through the paschal mystery we have been buried with Christ in baptism, so that we may rise with him to newness of life" (RCIA, 237).

Helping teens understand God's sharp tooth and God's loving kindness in their lives and helping them experience that place beyond, where there is peace, is not possible outside this paschal mystery. One asks them: Have you ever known a night so long and dark that morning never came? Is your story finished? There have been many deaths on a cross and Easter mornings, and there will be more.

THE PASCH IS CELEBRATED THROUGH THE CHURCH CALENDAR

Throughout the year, the faithful mark the paschal journey Sunday by Sunday, season by season, feast by feast, but most of all in the Paschal Triduum. How can teens live that mystery through the church calendar? By immersion from infancy in a domestic church, a base community, a parish and a universal ecclesial setting that takes that mystery and that calendar seriously. Outside that setting, rites and customs are phony, catechesis is meaningless, religious education is an empty mental exercise and social action can be aimless. The ecclesial setting—whatever its shape: peer, interest, ethnic, school, economic, neighborhood, household, parish, metropolitan, national or inter-national—must be that of the body of Christ.

Some teens resonate with certain elements of the church calen-dar; others resonate with other elements. Usually teens can be helped to group themselves according to interests, and if an interest group has a competent facilitator—such as the apprentice/master model—then skills can be developed, experiments worked, praise given, wounds healed, insight gained, information learned and events celebrated. Groups may focus on poetry, music, crafts, art, parties, sports, drama, prayer, folk religious practice, folk customs, ethics, dance, food, health, career, works of justice and peace. The RCIA can touch all of these with teens, and all of these can touch the paschal mystery of Christ.

To Be or
Not to Be
a Christian

J. LEO KLEIN

S EVERAL YEARS AGO at Xavier University in Cincinnati, the
department of theology and the campus ministry staff cospon-
sored a program given for academic credit titled "To Be or Not to Be a
Christian."

All undergraduate students at Xavier are required, as a part of
their liberal arts core curriculum, to take four courses in theology.
These courses are geared to a student's understanding of theological
issues and do not deal directly with a student's religious identity or
specifically religious growth. "To Be or Not to Be a Christian,"
however, took a brave step in the direction of integrating theological
knowledge and religious identity and growth. This course was
properly described ahead of time to prospective participants so that
they would understand what they were getting into and would be free
to choose a course that offered a heavier agenda than the average
course in theology with which they were accustomed. They realized
that the course would deal with their own religious commitment and
they were free to take it or leave it.

This course was founded on a pastoral theology that realized that infant baptism was no guarantee that the young adult would embrace the faith in which he or she had been baptized. So much would depend on whether, over the years of childhood and adolescence, the young person had the opportunity for development in faith. Such an adult commitment depended as well on whether the gift of faith still remained in the person's mind and heart by the late teens and early 20s. The course was to be an adventure in education and an adventure in discernment.

Unconditional Personal Support

The prospective participant in our program was encouraged to see, from the beginning, that the teachers were leaders and facilitators but the ultimate decision about whether one found oneself with Christian faith would be one's own perception. If a student came to the conclusion that he or she was agnostic or atheist, he or she would not be judged negatively. The object of the course was "discovery," which would lead to conclusions about the religious directions of one's life. A student would expect an academic grade in this course but the grade (Pass or Fail) would be determined on the seriousness with which one cooperated with the course structures and not on the conclusions about one's religious identity.

The teachers for the course represented a cross section of personnel from the ministry staff and from the theology faculty. They were committed to work as a team and engaged in long hours of planning before the course began and during the progress of the course. A presentation of Christian faith and life formed the outline of the course content, but the reactions of the students to the presentation was a crucial factor in adjusting the content to the students and adapting it to their pastoral needs.

Structures

We limited the course to 36 students. Each of the six teachers was responsible for six of the students. In addition to the twice-weekly evening sessions of two hours for the entire group, each teacher had a weekly interview of an hour with each of those six students. Each student kept a journal during the course and shared its contents with the teacher during the weekly conference.

The course ran for the seven weeks before Easter and included a weekend away from campus at a local retreat house as well as time spent together for the Paschal Triduum. It continued for another seven weeks after Easter.

We started by looking for students for whom faith in God and/or in Jesus was a critical issue. Some serious degree of agnosticism was a course requirement. Members of the teaching staff interviewed every candidate for the course. The interview and an assessment of agnosticism was necessary before the student received permission to register for the course. A number of students were turned down for the course because they were clearly committed Christians.

That is the theory and structure of the course. Some anecdotes, taken together, tell the story of "To Be or Not to Be a Christian" as a learning experience for both teachers and students.

Few of the students were previously acquainted with others who would be in the course with them. We planned a social get-together some days before the first official session of the course. After a welcome, a few brief announcements and introductions of the six teachers and 36 students to each other, the rest of the evening was spent enjoying relaxed conversation and pizza. One soft-spoken senior confided to me that the prospect of the course brought him great relief. For years, he had worried about what seemed to him his total absence of faith. He did not bring the matter up with his parents because such questioning "might hurt them." Nor did he broach the matter with any of his friends because he felt his questions might scandalize them and disturb the faith they all seemed to have. "You can imagine," he said, "how great it is to be here in a room with 35 others who feel the same way I do."

The regular twice-weekly class sessions were planned by the staff and combined lecture, whole-group discussion, individual reflection or written reactions to presentations and discussion by each of the small groups with its faculty facilitator. The rhythm was varied.

Process of Discernment

At one of the early class sessions, I was with my small group of six as each one shared some personal background with the others in the group. One group member was telling the rest of us in rather intimate detail about some of his life's escapades that in no way redounded to his personal credit. I remember remarking to myself at the trust he was putting in others he hardly knew. All of a sudden he stopped his story and spoke in surprise: "Hey, do you know I'm telling you all things I've never told anyone else before! Well, as I was saying . . ." And he continued with his personal narrative. The others gave him undivided attention and, as I think he realized, real, unspoken support.

Our staff of teachers asked ourselves each week as we planned ahead, "Well, where are they now? Are they ready for more content or do we need more time to mull over with them what already has been presented?" And so we gradually moved through questions about the existence of God, the meaning of faith, the person of Jesus. We were committed as a group to see that "content" issues never would force us to move more quickly than the group of students could manage.

During one of our planning sessions, we were each reporting to the other teachers on where we thought our group of students was at that point. Based on this shared reading of the group of students, the next step usually had presented itself to us up to that time. One of the teachers reported that the intellectual content of what we had presented thus far in the course was quite clear to his group. But it was becoming evident to him and to several of his six students that to move ahead with this journey would require some serious moral conversion in their lives. They simply could not go where the course seemed to be calling them while they were wedded to this or that pattern of behavior in their lives. This teacher offered to meet separately with his group until they moved past the impasse. What occurred to all of us was the need for prayer and fasting for these students, and we quietly committed ourselves to a regimen of prayer and fasting to support moral conversion and strength of faith in the students. That was something we had not counted on when we began the enterprise.

On another occasion at a planning session, we found ourselves confused about how to proceed. We had plenty of content with which to move ahead, but we also had serious doubts about where the students found themselves. One of the teachers suggested that we break our logjam by simply telling the students the facts: We didn't know how to proceed. We formed a panel of teachers and, one by one, reported to the students on the difficulties we were having "reading" them. At first they seemed surprised at this, but in a very short time we had a wonderful discussion going in a common discernment of where, as a matter of fact, the students did find themselves.

Not only did that honesty on the part of the teachers break the logjam, but one of the students told me weeks later that it was the best class of the entire course because, as he said, "It showed us you were really listening to us." He suggested that if, in future courses, we ever should develop a syllabus with certain topics tied to a given evening class, that is when we should stop giving this course.

We discovered as the course proceeded that one of the most common blocks to believing for these students was a distorted image of God. This could have resulted from a poor catechetical formation early in life or from the conclusions about God that a given young person made because of things that had happened to her or him in the course of life. One of the most warm and pleasant young people in my group eventually unfolded for me a tragic dimension of her family history: the serious results of her father's alcoholism. She came to say aloud (she admitted, for the first time in her life) how very angry she was with her parent and how angry she was with God who was responsible for all the suffering. I asked her to tell me who she thought this God was, what God was like. The picture she had drawn for herself, the conclusions she had come to about God, were nowhere near the God of the Christian scriptures. I told her honestly that I never could believe in the God she described and saw why she had trouble with faith. That night we began a gradual presentation of the God of the Christians so that she could see whether or not she was called to believe in that God.

Some Ritual Activity

At a later stage, when the group was considering Christian life, life in the church, we devoted an evening to a consideration of eucharist. By definition, this group was not ready to participate in a real eucharist, but we wanted to talk about eucharist and then show them what it could be like. After some lectures about eucharist, we invited them to act out eucharist. The acting came near the end of the evening session when the concentration of the students was diminishing. I was concerned that the model eucharist might not prove effective. That concern was in vain.

All of us sat around a long table covered with sheets to resemble a big dining-room table. I said the words of a eucharistic prayer over a huge loaf of homemade wheat bread and a large cup of rosé wine. The only lighting in the room was candlelight. Once the words of the eucharistic prayer were concluded, I broke the bread and passed it around among the "diners," followed by an invitation to share from the cup. Each student received a big hunk of delicious bread, which he or she had to eat. And the drink of wine was no small sip because they needed the wine to wash down the bread. They realized from the lecture earlier in the evening that sharing in the bread and cup meant eating and drinking one's way into the sentiments expressed in the blessing prayer.

As we finished this acting out of the eucharistic rite, it was getting late. I told them we now could go in peace. They all just sat there in what seemed a stunned silence. The rite captivated them and only after a second invitation to depart did they get up and leave the room, for the most part, in silence.

On another occasion, ritual played an important part in learning. Our group was together from noon to three o'clock on Good Friday. The purpose was to concentrate on the suffering and death of Jesus to help the students assess their own reactions to this part of the Christian proclamation.

We rounded up a used set of the 14 stations of the cross, wooden plaques that had hung in a small chapel on campus. Fourteen students volunteered to take one station apiece and we all went our separate ways for an hour to think about the story of the passion. When we reconvened, each student who had one of the stations was responsible for presenting this station to the rest of us for our reflection. The student could use any device he or she wanted. Their imaginations were extraordinary!

The most moving presentation for me was given by a young man who took the 11th station, "Jesus is nailed to the cross." He had us all lie down flat on our backs and close our eyes while he led us in fantasy through the nailing down of my left foot, my right foot, my left hand, my right hand. As each member was fastened to the cross, the young man reminded us what we were giving up, what we now could no longer do. And Jesus went through this for us. No stations of the cross I had ever made came near the intensity of that afternoon.

Where did it all end? Many of the 36 students found themselves within the Christian faith by the end of the course. Several of them renewed their baptismal promises at the Easter Vigil. Some remained agnostic. One young man admitted at the end of the course that he knew now for sure that he was agnostic but the big difference was that he no longer felt guilty about that. He wasn't sure about his future: He allowed that he might someday find himself with the gift of faith, but not yet.

Afterthoughts

The course consumed a great amount of time and energy for the staff of teachers. All felt, however, that the department of theology and the campus ministry staff was well served by the program. When it was announced the next year that the course would be repeated, there was a ready group of applicants.

Though most of the students in the class had been baptized as infants, they needed the freedom—and the permission—to ask any question they desired. Their past experiences—religious or otherwise—played a much greater part in their religious development than they had imagined.

I suspect there are far more baptized agnostics out there than we think. They need unconditional personal support, structures, a process of discernment and perhaps to experience some ritual activity to own or disown their Christian identity and the implications of that identity for their lives in the years ahead. That's what I think it takes for many young people to decide whether to be or not to be a Christian.

Rekindling the Gift of God in Youth

CAROL AND LARRY NYBERG

A S WE AGONIZE over the exodus of teenagers from the church, could it be that the church first has left them? Have we searched enough to find food for their growing, stretching hearts? There is something vital yet vexing about the period of adolescence, as there is about the preschool years. At both stages of development, children are caught up in a ferment of discovery and self-awareness and they instinctively push and test the limits they perceive that others are setting for them. Both groups of children are ripe for something that for the most part we have not bothered to identify.

Adolescence is the period of passage to adulthood. The cultural ubiquity of rites of passage celebrating puberty testifies to the natural significance of this period. The cultural gravity of this passage may have pulled the Christian rite of confirmation gradually toward an age that cries out so dramatically for attention. Given the "accidental" separation of confirmation from baptism (for example, the delay of bishops' visitations or the apologetic nature of religious education that crept into sacramental catechesis), why not put it at adolescence?

Rite of Passage

If we look at another rite of passage that recognizes the realms of both nature (puberty) and grace (journey of faith), we may find clues or analogies to what the church can offer teenagers during this period in their lives. The bar mitzvah has been a traditional part of the Jewish culture since the Middle Ages, but even this has antecedents and even older roots in the forms of prayers for children. Originally scheduled according to the appearance of physical signs of adolescence, the age later became formalized at 13 and one day for boys, 12 and one day for girls. Do we have anything to learn about how to celebrate and support our youth in this period of their life cycle?

> Bar Mitzvah is an act that brings the child's early years to formal conclusion. At the same time, it publicly opens a new chapter in life. The boys and the girls are about to enter adolescence, a difficult period. In many ways they are still children, but increasingly they wish to be recognized as adults. And they wish to know how parents and society view them. Judaism tells them where they belong: True, they are still dependents, but in the context of religious life, as participants in worship, they are adults. They have to assume the burdens that go with adulthood and can equally claim the respect that is due an adult. They know where they stand.[1]

Here are some elements we would do well to consider in our search for solutions to the problem of adolescent formation:

- the end of childhood but not of dependence
- the importance for teenagers to know how they are viewed by their parents, the larger church and all of society
- the need on the part of teenagers to answer questions about where they belong and where they stand in the community, based not on attaining some elusive "maturity" but rather on reaching the age of puberty
- the transition to adult participation in worship
- the assumption of new responsibility in religious life

Even if everyone could agree that these elements are worth marking, full awareness and commitment in adolescents do not just happen at a prescribed time. Rather, they require preparation from an early age. Children need roots in Christ, grounding in the church and ownership of the place where they meet: the liturgy. Proper preparation throughout the developmental years means that by adolescence these foundations will have become firm enough to be reflected on and built on.

In recent years, we have begun to see that for all of us life continues along the lines of the catechumenate. Although we will never be catechumens again, we will continue to journey in faith throughout our lives. Attention to this journey is given in the shape of the church year, which in large measure was generated by the demands of the catechumenate. What follows is an outline of the formation of young persons through adolescence that attempts to draw them into this journey.

Preadolescent Formation

The incorporation of children born into the family of faith, the journey of these particular children of God, should begin at conception and move toward baptism with the preparation of the parents and godparents and with the community witnessing and promising to support these persons in their life in Christ.[2] After baptism-chrismation-eucharist, the children's pilgrimage continues each week as they participate in the communal meal and, as receivers of the gift of Christ in the eucharist, are witnesses of faith to the congregation.[3] As they grow, they are invited from the youngest possible age into the larger family through the stories of scripture and meditations on the mysteries of the liturgy.[4]

As they approach the traditional age of first communion, elementary-school children are offered more intentional formation in the meaning of communion and community and on the gift of reconciliation. During this phase of formation, several values drawn from the insights of the restored catechumenate can be shared with the children: praying for them in the intercessions of the congregation, presentation of the gospel, creed, Lord's Prayer. They are not catechumens, but, as partakers in the mysteries, the children are offered times of mystagogical reflection—an intense consideration of the events they have experienced and the meaning of those events in their lives.

Adolescence brings a search for identity and affiliation. The community of faith now must claim the teenagers as its own and support them in their journey. Youth ministers tell of the isolation from the church community that they and the teens sometimes feel. Although the teenagers may appear to welcome the isolation and often deride attempts to include them, it is important for them to be made a part of the community. They must know that they are wanted and esteemed.

Rekindle the Gift of God within You

> I thank God whom I serve with a clear conscience, as did my ancestors, when I remember you constantly in my prayers. As I remember your tears, I long night and day to see you, that I may be filled with joy. I am reminded of your sincere faith, a faith that dwelt first in your grandmother Lois and your mother Eunice and now, I am sure, dwells in you. Hence I remind you to rekindle the gift of God within you through the laying on of my hands; for God did not give us a spirit of timidity but a spirit of power, love and self-control. (2 Timothy 1:3–7)

The advice to Timothy suggests a reality that we may have ignored: the need for intentional renewing or rekindling of the gifts that we received at baptism-chrismation-eucharist. It also presents us with a pattern that seems to be shared by all sacramental rites in one way or another. Using the terminology of the eucharist, we always find *anamnesis* (remembering) and *epiclesis* (invoking the Holy Spirit). *Anamnesis* is more than remembering, however; it is making present the reality of the past. It is recollection in the most literal sense: gathering oneself and one's past together at this moment to reconstitute the whole in the present. *Epiclesis,* a calling of the Holy Spirit in sacramental rites, includes a gesture of the hands.

So Paul recalls his love for Timothy, the faith they share and Timothy's own gifts. Paul reminds Timothy who and whose he is. Then he calls Timothy to remember how he was given those gifts by the laying on of hands, a gesture of *epiclesis*. Paul charges Timothy to rekindle those gifts so that they will not be used timidly but in power, love and self-control.[5] This suggests a way of celebrating an adolescent child's entrance into a new stage of life in the church.

Anamnesis

A period of *anamnesis* (remembering, contextualizing) offers candidates an opportunity to discover anew where they belong and where they stand within the family, the local community and the communion of saints. Ideally, this period may last for one liturgical (or school) year and may begin at age 12 or 13. Drama, art, storytelling, interviewing members of the parish, films, videos and field trips can help enliven a journey through the history of the faith.

THEY REFLECT ON THEIR OWN LIVES OF FAITH

By recalling together their baptism–chrismation–eucharist, formation, reconciliation, healing as well as special family events such as deaths and births, the candidates trace their pilgrimage of faith. Catechists offer a meditation to help them recall times when God was with them but they did not realize it at first.

THEY RESEARCH A SPECIAL SAINT

Perhaps the solemnity of All Saints may provide an opportunity for candidates to research the life of a saint they admire or are named after.

THEY STUDY GOD'S LOVE FOR ISRAEL AND THE CHURCH

From Advent through Lent, activity may focus on a survey of the history of God's people in the Jewish and Christian scriptures. This activity may best follow the Sunday lectionary readings by helping the candidates to place events in proper historical or social context.

THEY OBSERVE THE SACRED TRIDUUM

As a group within the larger community, they pray, celebrate the liturgy, fast, participate in mission, receive catechesis on the paschal mystery, observe the days according to local customs.

DURING EASTER'S 50 DAYS, THEY CELEBRATE THE CHURCH

Eastertime affords the candidates an opportunity to look at the history of Christianity through the Acts of the Apostles. Their catechesis during this time is oriented to the tradition of the church, especially through the eucharistic life of prayer and good works.

Catechesis for Ministry

After the period of *anamnesis,* the young teenagers have an opportunity to choose whether they want to move on to a period of ministry, another one-year period. Because the readings change over the three-year lectionary cycle, the content of the catechesis varies.

THEY VIEW SACRAMENTS IN THE LIGHT OF MINISTRY

The group considers the questions, "How are we called to ministry and how are we empowered for it?"[6] They explore the liturgical signs related to ministry—gestures, water, oil, light, vesture (the baptismal garment especially).

THEY DISCERN THEIR OWN GIFTS

Through prayer, reflection and discussion, they look at the needs of the community and their own strengths. A junior-high retreat recently offered in the Episcopal diocese of Chicago functioned well for this purpose. The retreat, called "Feast,"[7] was an experience of the church year over one weekend that brought it alive as proclamation, story and encounter with Christ. The participants shared experiences freely and expressed eagerness for another such event.

THEY EXPLORE MINISTRIES

First, they name the ministries closest to them: their participation in their families, their roles as students, their responsibility to their peers. They are affirmed in those vital and highest-ranking ministries and they are called to rekindle their commitment in them.

Second, they research the ministries of justice and peace in their own parish, in their own diocese or among other churches and groups. With the help of family and catechists, individually or in small groups, the teenagers choose a ministry to explore by serving in it for a time. Each is paired with one or several adult or family sponsors who already are committed to the same ministry.

These adults or families are supported by the parish throughout the period of their ministry as sponsors. They meet together regularly for direction and prayer.

Epiclesis

On Pentecost, the 50th day of Easter, the young teenagers are sent out by the community, empowered for their chosen ministry. They commit themselves to this ministry for a specific period of time, perhaps a year. The empowering consists in the laying on of hands accompanied by words of affirmation. This action and these words recall the young person's Christian initiation and indicate the community's commissioning.

Working side by side in the ministry, the young persons and their adult and family sponsors discover opportunities for mutual Christian formation. All need ongoing support. This rite and commitment to ministry for a given period of time can be repeated throughout adolescence as the teenagers search for their place in the reign of God.

The young persons also must be included actively in the community's liturgy on a regular basis if the empowering for mission is to have continued meaning. Ministries of hospitality for parish liturgies, for example, as well as catechetical or liturgical ministries with younger children can serve a reciprocally supportive function.

Celebration of Ministry

One possible rite, adapted from the commissioning for ministries in the Episcopal *Book of Occasional Services,* is as follows.

This rite may be used following the homily of the eucharistic liturgy on Pentecost Sunday or another Sunday. If it takes place outside that context, one of the following scripture texts or another suitable text is read:

1 SAMUEL 3:1—14 *The call of Samuel*
PSALM 103 *Praise of divine goodness*
2 TIMOTHY 1:3—14 *Paul urges Timothy to rekindle God's gift*
LUKE 2:41—52 *Jesus in the temple*

After the young persons are called forward, each is presented individually to the assembly by an adult sponsor. The presider reflects briefly on the period of anamnesis *that the young persons have experienced, on their discernment of needs and gifts and on their exploration of possible ministries.*

The presider continues:

As we remember the lives of these persons before us, let us also renew our commitment to them that began at their baptism.

To parents, godparents and sponsors:

Will you by your prayers and witness help this person continue to grow into full stature in Christ?

Parents, godparents and sponsors:

I will with God's help.

And to the congregation:

Will you who witness these vows do all in your power to support these persons in their life in Christ?

Congregation:

We will.

CREED OR RENEWAL OF THE BAPTISMAL COVENANT

[*For texts see the* Book of Common Prayer, *304–5, or* Rite of Christian Initiation of Adults, *238–39.]*

The congregation is seated. The presider stands in full view of the people. The sponsors and young persons stand facing the presider.
The presider says these or similar words:

Brothers and sisters, we all are baptized by the one Spirit into the one body and given gifts in a variety of ministries for the common good. Our purpose is to commission these persons in the name of God and of this congregation to a special ministry to which they are called.

The presider asks the sponsors:

Are these persons you present prepared by a commitment to Christ as Lord, by regular participation in worship and by knowledge of their duties, to exercise their ministry to the honor of God and the benefit of the church?

Sponsors:

They are.

The presider then says these or similar words:

You have been called to a ministry by God and this assembly. Will you, as long as you are engaged in this work, perform it with diligence?

Young persons:

I will.

Presider:

Will you reverently execute the duties of your ministry to the honor of God and the benefit of the world?

Young persons:

I will.

THE COMMISSIONING

Sponsors individually:

> I present *N.* to you to be admitted to the ministry of *N.*

Presider for each individual:

> In the name of God and of this assembly, I bless you, *N.*, for the ministry of *N.*

The presider invites the sponsors, parents and adult members of the assembly to join in the laying on of hands as together they pray for the young ministers:

Presider:

> Again and again in ages past, O God, you have called all people to serve you. You called the boy Samuel and prepared him to be a prophet for your people Israel. While David was a youth watching over his family's flock, you set him apart and anointed him king.
>
> You called the Blessed Virgin Mary, while still a young woman, to bear your Son, Jesus. As you blessed Mary with your Holy Spirit, bless these young people also, that they, like Samuel, may bring your word to those they serve. May they be filled with your love like David. May your gift be rekindled in them, Lord God, by the laying on of our hands, that they serve others with a spirit of power, love and eagerness for the coming of your reign from heaven. And like your Son, our Lord Jesus Christ, may they grow in wisdom and in stature and in favor with you and all creation. We ask this through Christ our Lord.

All:

> Amen.

The Sunday liturgy continues with the general intercessions. One or more of the new ministers may lead the petitions.

Notes

1. Leo Trepp, *The Complete Book of Jewish Observance: A Practical Manual for the Modern Jew* (New York: Behrman House/Summit Books, 1980), 242.

2. See Gail Ramshaw-Schmidt, "Celebrating Baptism in Stages: A Proposal," *Alternative Futures for Worship 2: Baptism and Confirmation* (Collegeville: The Liturgical Press, 1987), 137–55.

3. In Episcopal churches the practice of infant communion is gradually returning, primarily because of the recognition of the 1979 *Book of Common Prayer* that baptism is full initiation into the church and that chrismation is to be included in the baptismal rite. See, for example, Leonel L. Mitchell, "The Communion of Infants and Little Children," *The Anglican Theological Review* 71 (Winter 1989), 63–78; cf. Ramshaw-Schmidt, "Celebrating Baptism," 152. Although current Catholic practice presents obstacles to infant communion, it was once a normative practice. In the early *Roman Orders* (Ordines Romani), confirmation still depended exclusively on the bishop, but when he was present for the combined initiatory rites, the communion of infants followed immediately. See also the rubric from the twelfth-century *Pontifical,* cited in A. G. Martimort, *The Church at Prayer 3: The Sacraments* (Collegeville: The Liturgical Press, 1988), 70. The suggestions outlined here, however, easily can be adapted to a pattern of delayed confirmation and first communion.

4. For a sensitive and successful attempt to introduce young children to the deepest realities of the faith through engagement with scripture and liturgy, see Sofia Cavalletti, *The Religious Potential of the Child* (New York: Paulist Press, 1983).

5. Here the laying on of hands may refer to Timothy's ordination (cf. 1 Timothy 4:14). But two factors suggest the appropriateness of the application we recommend here: The primary sacrament of ministry is baptism and, though the laying on of hands has many functions in both Bible and liturgy, it always signifies an invocation of the Holy Spirit.

6. The "Outline of Faith" in the *Book of Common Prayer* answers the question "Who are the ministers of the church?" with this response: "The ministers of the church are laypersons, bishops, priests and deacons."

7. Developed by John Dally, youth minister for the Episcopal diocese of Chicago.

Ambassadors of Reconciliation

JACQUELYN MALLORY

PERHAPS *RECONCILIATION* rather than *confirmation* more suits the realities of life for teens. Young people can be some of the most-alienated and alienating people around and at the same time they can be some of the most reconciled and reconciling. Their power to reconcile exceeds that of most other age groups and that fact deserves reflection. As Paul the apostle put it, "We are ambassadors for Christ, as if God were appealing through us; we implore you on behalf of Christ, be reconciled to God" (2 Corinthians 5:20).

My Word, My Self, My Gift

José Hobday, a Franciscan sister, tells how a group of Native American youngsters search for their identity. Around the age of 12 or 13, they are sent out into the wilderness, apart from the family and tribe, to seek their Word. They find their Word by listening to the Great Spirit. When the Great Spirit speaks their Word to them, they return to the tribe to live now as their Word (e.g., "love," "courage," "compassion," "peace," "justice"). The Word must never pass their lips but must be lived in such a way that everyone in the tribe knows them by their Word. Their Word is a gift to the community, contributing word to sentence, then to paragraph, then to the community's story.

This is every adolescent. They seek an identity that can give motivation and purpose to life. Searching, they are estranged from family and community. For today's teens, this search often looks quite chaotic. David Elkind has described this in *All Grown Up and No Place To Go*.[1] We have removed the markers that once assured children that they have space and time to search out their identity. Losing intimacy with family, school and church community, many inappropriately substitute such things as gangs, drugs, cults or eating disorders as "safe places" in which to find themselves. It is always a time of alienation. But what sort of alienation?

Through baptism we are initiated into a life of reconciliation. That life is nourished and committed in sharing eucharist together. By joining the adult members at the eucharist, children and young people accept that commitment. Thus all members of the Christian community are called to holiness, to hold, live and share faith and reconciliation. Paul captured it: "This means that if anyone is in Christ, that person is a new creation. The old order has passed away; now all is new! All this has been done by God, in Christ, who has reconciled us through Christ and has given us the ministry of reconciliation" (2 Corinthians 5:17–18). If many adult members have not appropriated their Christian identity, are not living their "Word," what can we expect of adolescents, whose task it is to search? It seems we often are confirming faith in teens who still are in the wilderness, waiting on the Holy Spirit for their Word. Confirmations are not appropriate for wilderness wanderings nor for returning home. I suggest that reconciliation is.

Reembracing

Jesus tells the story of a man who had two sons. The younger seeks his identity by taking his share of the inheritance and leaving the farm. Along the way, he "finds himself" to be a broken youth in a strange place. The older son works out his identity by staying. He, too, finds himself to be broken when his brother returns to his father's embrace and a lavish celebration. The wise father recognizes the need for reconciliation and rejoicing: "My son, you are with me always, and everything I have is yours. But we had to celebrate and rejoice! This brother of yours was dead, and has come back to life. He was lost, and is found."

Paul Pearsall, in *The Power of the Family: Strength, Comfort, and Healing,* describes the family reembracement ritual this way:

> Their own problems are so severe that they seem for a time to be gone, departed for their own private journey that can teach them even as it stresses them. They become focused away from family, in toward their own issues. The family member returns from such quests a different person, with different feelings and perceptions of the world that can help the family grow only if all of the other family members can come to understand some of these experiences. Like a traveler returned from a long and arduous voyage, the returning member can help the family grow by bringing new and challenging experiences back into the family system. But to do so requires a return to family ritual to allow a smooth reentry.[2]

Such a ritual would seem to be needed as adolescents negotiate their identity quest and return renewed to the Christian community. Hence, we once again share the peace and meaning of the community with each other, renewing our baptism by celebrating and rejoicing at the eucharist, being sent once again in ministry to the world. We identify ourselves again as ambassadors for Christ. Reconciliation accomplishes this in the community.

Reconciliation and initiation are closely linked. The laying on of hands in penance as in confirmation offers a glimpse of that link. In the history of Christianity, the laying on of hands carried these two meanings: restoring a penitent to the community and thus the eucharistic table and moving the baptized from the font to the eucharistic table. The practice of each sacrament changed over time. Penance now would seem to be the transitory sacrament. This laying on of hands, like the family reembracement ritual, speaks of healing the divisions before a member comes to a new identity in the community. Such rituals also confer blessing and affirm the way one will live out this new identity.

Companions on the Way

In Nineveh, Tobit and Anna have a son, Tobiah. Tobit, who walks the path of righteousness and fidelity to God, is blinded by cataracts. In another city, Raguel and Edna have a daughter, Sarah, who had the misfortune of having seven successive husbands die on their wedding night. It seems the demon, Asmodeus, desires Sarah for himself. Tobiah is the instrument of healing for both families. His companion on the journey is the angel, Raphael, whose name means "God heals." Raphael guides Tobiah on the journey where he will marry his kinswoman, Sarah. Raphael teaches him the healing technique he will need for both families, secures the demon so that Tobiah is protected from the fate of Sarah's seven previous husbands and brings them both back to Tobit and Anna where Tobiah curses his father's blindness. All rejoice in God's mercy.

Teens need "Raphael companions" along the journey to guide, teach, protect and secure demons and to bring the teens back home. The vision quest leads to identity and to vocation. Our teens are disenchanted by our own lackluster response to the great mission. They long for a quest equal to their idealism and energy. Episcopal theologian John Westerhoff says that we are more likely to act our way into believing than to believe our way into acting. We are sent to act, to heal each other. Like the 72 in Luke's story of the great commissioning (Luke 10:1–22), we often are sent out in pairs. Teens will question the sacrament of penance, as they do the sacrament of confirmation, if they do not have companions and practitioners of reconciliation for the journey.

We have such companions in our midst. They are those who have made the journey themselves and have returned to embrace the mission and ministry of Jesus. They are the communion of saints. Some have performed ordinary things remarkably well. Baptismal sponsors might be lifelong companions. An admired family member might be that companion. We might be surprised at who turns out to be a guardian angel. We all enter into the penitential life at baptism and we all have stories of companioning others into wholeness and healing. At the end of the Lucan passage, Jesus tells the returning disciples that he saw the things that had been accomplished by their going out in pairs: "At that moment Jesus rejoiced in the Holy Spirit."

Implications

From these stories come a few observations. I suggest we reestablish adolescence as that time and space where family, friends and community permit, affirm and encourage young people to search for their personal word, their identity. We should not be hurrying them along. The sacrament of penance can play a part in this growth and seeking, as well as in the reembracing and enabling that makes people both the reconciled and reconcilers.

Opportunities abound throughout the church year to reembrace teenagers and to enable them to be ambassadors of reconciliation.[3] An evangelizing catechesis, for example, during the season of Lent can lead powerfully to teen involvement in the Paschal Triduum in which reconciliation has a special place.

If we continue to celebrate this sacrament as integral to the movement from baptism and eucharist to vocation, then we need to take seriously the role of companion. Teenagers today need companions from the community who can help them negotiate the journey. We must provide the guides, protectors, healers, teachers and visionaries; the world is all too willing to do so in our absence.

Let us live in the joyful hope that it can be said of us that we live our Word so intentionally that it never need pass our lips and yet people will know us.

Notes

1. David Elkind, *All Grown Up and No Place to Go: Teenagers in Crisis* (Reading MA: Addison-Wesley, 1984), 4–10.

2. Paul Pearsall, *The Power of the Family: Strength, Comfort, and Healing* (Garden City NY: Doubleday and Co., Inc., 1990), 47 f.

3. Patrick J. Brennan, in *The Reconciling Parish: A Resource for Parish Staffs and Leaders* (Allen TX: Tabor Publishing, 1990), offers several suggestions for processes, rites and reflections that may appeal to teenagers.